WHAT ARE YOUR KIDS READING?

WHAT ARE YOUR KIDS READING?

THE ALARMING TREND IN TODAY'S TEEN LITERATURE

JILL CARLSON

Wolgemuth & Hyatt, Publishers, Inc.
Brentwood, Tennessee

The mission of Wolgemuth & Hyatt, Publishers, Inc. is to publish and distribute books that lead individuals toward:

- A personal faith in the one true God: Father, Son, and Holy Spirit;

- A lifestyle of practical discipleship; and

- A worldview that is consistent with the historic, Christian faith.

Moreover, the Company endeavors to accomplish this mission at a reasonable profit and in a manner which glorifies God and serves His Kingdom.

Wolgemuth & Hyatt, Publishers, Inc.
1749 Mallory Lane, Suite 110
Brentwood, Tennessee 37027

Library of Congress Cataloging-in-Publication Data

Carlson, Jill.
    What are your kids reading? : the alarming trend in today's teen
literature / Jill Carlson. — 1st ed.
        p.   cm.
    Includes bibliographical references and index.
    ISBN 1-56121-072-2
    1. Teenagers—Books and reading. 2. High school libraries.
I. Title.
Z1037.A1C343 1991
028.5'35—dc20

91-18874
CIP

For Mother
She read to me.

And

For Andy, Class of 2004
I finished the book for him.

Contents

Acknowledgments

W hat my parents began in their fireside readings stuck: Except for my incredible sixteenth year, I would sooner have been without shoes than a book.

But for *this* project it took more than my love of books. I needed help. I can never finish thanking my husband, who wrote, encouraged, prayed, fixed computer crashes, and cooked his own supper. And my three grown kids—in fifteen minutes, they could critique with deadly insight pages which took me ten hours to create.

My readers. They finished each book and painstakingly churned out detailed reports. I promised them eight months of reading; they stuck with me for two years. Meetings. More meetings. And oh—not another book! Who are these incredible people?

- Kirk Bostwick. Secondary English teacher.

- Michael Brammer. Engineer with a major manufacturer.

- Jerry Carlson. Economics editor. Three children.

- Holly Crandall. Homemaker. Executive Committee, Board of Publications for her denomination. Four children.

- Ruth Ann Kachulis. Homemaker. Seminary student. Three children.

- Dan Manternach. Editor. Manager of market news publications for a national publishing firm. Two children.

- Hilda Ostby. Homemaker. Day-care operator. Five children.

- Janis Reisetter. Homemaker. Certified teacher. Three children.

- Juanita Ruby. Former owner, Christian bookstore. One step-child.

- Karen VandeKrol. Homemaker and home school teacher. Two children.

- Judy Walsten. Part-time preschool teacher. Homemaker. Two children.

- Elizabeth Curry Williams. Writer/editor. One child.

Legal counsel was freely given by Allen Wildmon of American Family Association and Alan Harkey of Lloyd Daniel Corporation. I am especially grateful to Judith A. Reisman, president, The Institute for Media Education, for hours of painstaking counsel.

And to these people I give grateful thanks for publishing, editing, and creative help: The editorial staff at Wolgemuth & Hyatt—for their great patience in answering question after question; Wendy Flint, National Educational Task Force; Pastor Andy Stymer of the Genesis Project; Sally Stuart of Christian Communicators; Paul Vitz, New York University; Phyllis Schlafly of *The Education Reporter*; Onalee McGraw of Educational Guidance Institute; Kathy Jacobs, Crossway Books; Jeannie Mikkelson, Bethany House; Barbara Mack, chief legal advisor for Iowa State University Journalism Department; and William G. Hendrick, advertising director, The Westminster/John Knox Press.

Teachers and librarians—overworked, underthanked—they took time for me. At our nearby Walnut Ridge Baptist Academy: Sarah Shepard, librarian; Pat Rosenberg, teacher. At Cedar Book Store, Marlene Wagenaar.

From Cedar Falls (Iowa) High School: Linda Waddle, librarian; from Ames (Iowa) High School: Karlene Garn. From the University of Northern Iowa: Norma Hassman, instructor in library science; Lucille Lettow, associate professor and youth librarian; Dr. Jeffrey Copeland, professor of English; Dr. Key Lee, professor of education.

Other help from around the country: Jeff Taylor, Indiana seminary student and former English teacher; Connie Espel, Illinois librarian; Forrest Turpen, executive director, Christian Educators Association, International; Jeannie Coulson (Mrs. William), from San Diego; Rev. Ken Farnham, from Cleveland, Oklahoma.

From the Hiawatha, Kansas, reading group: Staci Charles, day-care operator and former teacher; Mary Edwards; Debbie Heiniger; Dan Horton; Shirley Snavely; Mark Young. From the Kansas City, Missouri, reading group: Stephanie Carlson, dental assistant and freelance artist; Peter and Laurie Brook; Jack and Pat Matthews; Terry and Pam McCleave.

Many other librarians and English teachers courteously answered my unending questions.

For other research help I thank school superintendent Charles Clayton and Pastor Rick Conway of Cleveland, Oklahoma, and Iowa pastor Al Kuiper.

Rev. Ted Veer of Sudan Interior Mission and Bryce Christensen of The Rockford Institute gave valuable background information. My friend Phyllis Mortensen gave generously of time and resource books.

This project would have remained impaled on any of hundreds of obstacles without three solid years of faithful prayer by Dee Schildroth, our project prayer partner. For the same support, I also thank Bernie Huss, Helen Sneller, members of the young adult singles Bible-study group which meets in our home; Pastors Dan Munson and Bob Permenter and our church prayer groups; the Baileys—all of them; and the women in our "Moms in Touch" prayer support group.

But to the most important One: my prayers of thanks to the Lord. Without Him I would have loved my own words and not the Truth.

1

What Has Happened To Teen Fiction?

I t's midnight in Kansas City. Stephanie, a young dental assistant exhausted from a double-shift day, prepares to relax with the solace she learned as a child: a fascinating book filled with old friends.

Plumping her pillows, she settles back for chapter one. But this is the ninth book she's borrowed as part of a reading project on middle school library fiction. And tonight, she's not so sure she'll be in the company of friends.

With two exceptions, she finds that these new books are not peopled with the helpful characters and concepts she remembers from fifteen years ago. Instead, they're filled with ghosts and fourth-dimensional spirits, kids who are smarter than their parents, and a steady parade of weak authority figures. These nihilistic characters keep her awake and worried long after that particular book rests near her pillow.

Stephanie had volunteered to spearhead a parent reading project designed to check trends in teen fiction. Eager for the reading, she thought it would be fun to walk the halls again in memory—to be back smelling the new books, listening to lockers slam, watching the swishing bustle of kids.

But at project's end she had four pages of statistics showing why those books didn't fill her with the same delight she'd remembered. On behalf of her parent reading group she told the attentive and sympathetic librarian of her local middle school:

> These kids have real problems which the books claim to help. But these books don't give solid answers. They leave out the one ingredi-

1

ent my friends and their children lean on the most: a relationship with a personal and loving God, and a way of healing their hurts with His help. Sure, some of these kids come from broken homes. Some of them have never known a loving father. But what better reason to give these kids at least a small opportunity to read about a loving God.

To an astonished librarian she and her friends then donated $150 worth of God-centered books—some of which the kids at school had been asking for.

The Dominant Themes

Have *you* read the latest teen novels your kids get from the school library? You may be surprised, even shocked, at the values taught in those books. And not in just a few books. The problem exists in books which dominate major "recommended book" lists your public school librarians use to select novels for your high school, junior high, and middle-school kids.

That group of kids is called "young adults" by educators. We're told by these same educators these teenagers stagger under a mountain of problems—problems which these books are supposed to help solve. The books *do* give us problems—from death to peer pressure. But the answers are cloaked in a philosophy which gives very little room for the rights and wrongs you've been teaching your children—and a wide open door for kids to look within themselves for answers.

A group of parents in my community were so concerned about the concepts expressed by authors in teen novels that we began a three-year study.

First, the team read every word and statistically analyzed the content of forty-five books selected at random from the major lists of books recommended to librarians in 1988.

The Dominant Themes in Today's Teen Fiction

Here are the dominant themes of your kids' world as seen by today's teen authors in those forty-five books.

- Most fathers are absent or bad.
- 60 percent of mothers work outside the home full time.

- Marriage is boring or dangerous.
- Parents and their kids are estranged half the time.
- Clergy are bumbling hypocrites.
- The spirit world helps kids more than it hurts them.
- I can solve my own problems. God doesn't help.
- Minorities are unfairly represented.
- Sex outside marriage isn't wrong unless it's forced.
- Death is prominent, even pervasive.
- Profanity is in 70 percent of the books.

Profanity is a normal means of expression, as evidenced by the high percentage in these novels.

Those views of the world come packaged with superbly skilled writing and well-crafted conflicts designed to glue your teenager's eyes to the book.

But the dominant plots and authors' viewpoints lack diversity. Those one-sided themes often leave out the very values you've spent a lifetime

---

"Have you read the latest teen novels your kids get from the school library? You may be surprised, even shocked, at the values taught in those books."

---

teaching to your children. We found *no* books from Christian publishers on any recommended book list.

Next, other teams of adults did a similar analysis in four states. They chose books randomly from the 1988–90 purchases of one city high school, one middle school, one town library, and one city library.

We also browsed the places where you'll find 85 percent of all youth fiction—in university, small town, and city library youth sections. We checked and rechecked other recommended lists. Which books did experts rave over? Which books are on the "summer reading list"? Which books are showcased at librarian conferences? Which books and which authors show up in list after list?

We wanted to be sure the books we analyzed were a representative cross-section of the full spectrum offered in public teenage library sections today. We didn't select the "worst" books we could find. We made a scientifically random list, then checked it with other "best" lists.

For example, *New York Times* Children's Book Editor Eden Ross Lipson's list of the fifty "best young adult" (teen) books includes *five* novels out of the forty-five which we randomly chose for analysis. That's 10 percent of her list, which spans thirty years of publishing.[1]

Eighty-five percent of Nilsen and Donelson's prestigious Honors List in the 1987 column is *on our list!*[2]

In our visits to other American public libraries, we saw almost every book from the top-recommended group which we studied, some on special display. Book selections varied only slightly from one library to the next, probably reflecting the local librarian's judgment.

These observations come from a dozen parents who worked for two years, as well as other parent groups and libraries from four states. And it's clear that the pervasive viewpoints and values of this "new teenage fiction" are now on your teenagers' school or town library shelves and will be there to shape the moral development of new generations for another twenty to thirty years!

Repeated Themes in Public Libraries

In books from the middle school, profanity and sex were rare. But in both city and town public-library teen sections, up to 65 percent of the books contained profanity, and premarital sex was considered morally okay in half the situations portrayed.

Among those four community libraries, we saw these repeated themes:

- The spirit world is mysterious, dangerous, and fun.
- God is rarely mentioned. He is abstract and impersonal.
- Protagonists are usually white females.

- Teens take center stage. Little kids are barely mentioned, and older people are on the sidelines.

- Handicapps are rarely portrayed.

- Homemakers range from 18 percent to 60 percent positive.

- Half of all employment roles are white collar and self-employed. Only a third of these are portrayed negatively.

- Blacks are rarely mentioned, but never negatively.

- Profanity was in 45–65 percent of books in teen sections; 7 percent of middle-school books.

- Non-married sex is okay 50 percent of the times it was mentioned.

- Three books condone homosexual activity.

"In both city and town public-library teen sections, up to 65 percent of the books contained profanity, and premarital sex was considered morally okay in half the situations portrayed."

A Pervasive Problem

Like you, we love our kids and believe the ad campaigns that say, "Forget the TV and get out the books." We believe the slogans: "Reading is Fundamental" and "Readers are Leaders."

But the parents who carefully and objectively compiled thousands of statistics on these books are also Christians who love our Lord Jesus Christ. We want to read of His triumph and let our kids read about Him too. We want Him fairly represented in the diverse marketplace of modern fiction. And we want the choice of seeing how people of all races work through their problems with God's help. Almost without exception, novels which reveal God's positive power are censored from library shelves. Into this vacuum, today's teen authors pour a torrent of books offering a narrow spectrum of other "isms"—rationalism, occultism, and nihilism.

In the name of diversity, our kids are offered books channeling them into a humanistic dead end.

As a teen, I had access to public library books that didn't defame Christ, didn't rationalize teen sex as standard operating procedure, and didn't fill my head with obscene images.

In my suburban Washington D.C. high school of three thousand students, we studied the classics. I don't remember anyone telling me I had personal problems which "relevant" literature could solve! While I didn't realize it at the time, a good chunk of what I read was in line with Judeo-Christian principles. Those books reinforced what my parents taught me, rather than discrediting their values.

So I wasn't prepared for modern teenage "problem novels," drowning us in problems with no real solutions!

When I updated my English teaching certificate in 1986, I included a course in teen literature. I crashed into hundreds of new teen books and barely survived the impact. At semester end, our professor took a class tally of the books we'd studied. By show of hands we told him: In 90 percent of popular fiction, parents were morons, misfits, or molesters.

Had This New Brand of Fiction Reached the Public Schools?

I wondered.

I soon found out. I taught as a substitute English teacher for the next four years in two public junior highs, a public senior high school, a Catholic senior high, and one Christian elementary school.

The same books were in the public schools, all right. One weekend I dragged home six novels to prepare for Monday's teaching. The books focused on these conflicts:

- Verbally and physically abusive parents.
- A father who lets his son sleep with the female live-in houseguest.
- A mentally ill mother.

- An absent husband and a hostile father who ignores his son's achievements.

- Thrown in were five boys who steal their abusive father's car and storm across the country through alcohol abuse, "instant coffee" highs, and spotting girls on the pill (they do and they did and it's all described).

After my first year of substitute teaching, I challenged the head of a high school English department: Do teachers in independent reading units encourage balanced reading choices? The responses came in three stages:

- "You haven't spent 180 days in any of the classes. You can't know what you're talking about."

- "If you have a complaint, fill out a library censorship form."

- The third was to make sure I was never called again as a substitute teacher in that department.

But my challenge was *balance,* not censorship. Wasn't the first step in "critical thinking" to read a *wide variety?* Don't the new gurus of education preach *diversity?* So I did my own reading during "sub" days in other departments and other schools.

Read, Read, Read!

Junior high kids do a lot of free reading, and not just for English. Social studies and speech give fiction assignments too. "Library days" are common. There's a major effort to entice kids to *read.* Apparently, *what* is being read is not as important to many educators as the reading itself: Just get the kids to read *something!*

While I substituted, I saw other teachers give these free-reading fiction assignments:

1. Read everything you can by one author. Tell what's in the books. Do you like the author? Nothing you say about the book is right or wrong. Just *read.* (Lots of girls choose Judy Blume novels).

2. Read everything you can on one subject for one week. (Two years in a row I saw library carts for the in-class "Halloween

reading week"—with seventy-five books on occultism, ghosts, or psychic phenomena. "They're too depressing," one twelve-year-old told me. "I don't like them.")

3. Keep a running record of all the fiction books you read this year. (The idea is to read, read, read).

It was a paradox: Teachers with long track records of enthusiasm, award-winning skill, and student-bonding turned a blind side to the numbing, nihilistic flow of new values expressed in teen fiction. The change from earlier, morally sound fiction was so gradual that many teachers didn't realize the subtle shift.

That blind spot was one I could see in my own teaching and child-raising past: I thought for years that fiction's dual purpose was to beef up reading skills and to get kids to think critically. But it's more. Much more.

Fiction is a values factory, selling a product directly to your child. Much of pre-1965 fiction upholds Judeo-Christian values and other traditional ethics based on the concept of absolute right and wrong.

This inventory of older books in city *public* libraries provides a base which is gradually being diluted by the inflow from the "new-book" section. A few teachers resist the trend and stock heavily with pre-1965 paperbacks in their own classrooms!

But get a new-book library cart in your classroom, and you're likely to see ghosts as major characters, fathers as the modern bad guys, and ESP-skilled heroes who meditate. One beautifully-written new book about handicaps was ruined with a vengeance theme. A multiple-copy book used for both fourth and seventh grades was defended by administrators in one district as "meeting district guidelines" when publicly challenged for its minor profanity and privately challenged for its humanistic philosophy. When you see multiple-copy novels on a teacher's shelf, that's a signal it's widely popular or is assigned reading and it's almost impossible to "opt your child out" from such exposure.

Between subbing dates, I talk to parents. Only a few are even aware of the fiction their kids read at school.

The occasional parent who browses a page or two and finds it obscene or demonic is usually too intimidated by the school bureaucracy to protest. The librarian defends the choice under "freedom of information."

---

*"Teachers with long track records of
enthusiasm, award-winning skill, and
student-bonding turned a blind side to the
numbing, nihilistic flow of new values
expressed in teen fiction."*

One teacher who proudly announced to his class that he teaches "the twenty-five most banned books in American literature," became highly defensive when one parent asked him publicly where he got his list.

How Twelve Parents Got Involved

I thought about all those parents—and my own ignorance. That department head's comment kept coming back: "You don't know what you're talking about."

So I determined to know.

But I began naively: What if parents read the top fifty library checkouts from local high schools? If we tabulated how authors presented violence, profanity, race and handicaps, we'd write a stunning report in, oh, eight months tops.

Our state code lets any citizen check public records (except for *who's* checking out books). So I knew we had a right to know *how often* a given book had been checked out, as an index to how much impact each book had on its reading public.

But even with the state code before them, one school refused to reveal its most-read novels for three tense months. I wanted facts; they anticipated confrontation.

Another school cheerfully whipped out the computer list by return mail. The difference? I told the second high school I had "university help" with my project (I did, from very scientific professionals at the University of Northern Iowa). The first school became defensive when told "a group of parents" wanted to know what their kids were reading!

Those library readership lists were electrifying. (Stephen King books were 25 percent of one school's list and 3 percent of another, possibly because the first library had just had a "King Reading Contest.") But I felt they wouldn't represent the most reliable sample of what American kids are being offered to read today.

Computer rankings of books checked out most often don't show how much of the book is actually read. They don't say whether teachers or students read the books, or whether one student checks out twenty books while another reads one paragraph. And I knew better than to ask students for their favorite books. I had seen those English class questionnaires! Kids couldn't always remember what titles they had read. "Let's put *Garfield*," they snicker. And sure enough—it shows up on the influential "What Everybody's Reading" list.

After two months of poring over ERIC references (that's Educational Resources Information Center), my friend Holly Crandall suggested another way to get hard data. We could select randomly from "young adult" (teenage) marketing lists. These are the books selected by organizations of professional librarians. These books are the cream of the crop, the ones which reviewers urge teens to read *first!*

These books are promoted on lists, on posters, in review magazines— in senior highs, junior highs, middle schools, and the public library.

We double-checked by randomly asking 10 percent of Iowa's 450 high-school librarians where *they* get their purchase ideas. Twenty-seven schools responded, saying they use five main lists. Four national groups select the *very best books of each year and just about every librarian in the country has access to at least two of these lists by subscription.* The youth librarian at University of Northern Iowa confirmed that these lists (except "Iowa Teen Award") are tops everywhere.

Now we had our lists (see chapter 2). All were fiction promotionals from 1987 or 1988 for ages twelve to eighteen (called "young adults" by the education establishment). None were short stories or "series" books. Our forty-five books were from these lists:

1. American Library Association's "Best Books for Young Adults," published in *Booklist,* March 15, 1988.

2. *English Journal's* "Books for Young Adults Poll" (through University of Iowa, published nationally). *English Journal,* January, 1988.

3. Iowa Educational Media Association's "Iowa Teen Award," from the 1987–88 Masterlist (not tops in all states).

4. *School Library Journal's* "Books for Children and Young Adults," and "Best Adult Books for Young Adults," December, 1987.

5. *Booklist's* "Young Adults Editors' Choice." National Council of Teachers of English, January 14, 1988.

Which books are future classics? We won't know until they've been on the shelves twenty years. The forty-five books we analyzed were brand new, without the household blessing or curse of *To Kill a Mockingbird* or *The Catcher in the Rye*. We read them with fresh eyes and uncurdled stomachs.

"Even with the state code before them, one school refused to reveal its most-read novels for three tense months. I wanted facts; they anticipated confrontation."

Into our eighth month of reading and content analysis, our group of parents was like a woman hoping for labor to start. We had selected forty-five books by randomly assigned computer number from our lists. We had begun refining a six-page questionnaire which our University of Northern Iowa helper accepted as an objective means of analysis.

But we had only five books evaluated, and our twelve readers wondered what they'd gotten themselves into. We're readers, writers, and teachers. We knew what we wanted. How long could it take to finish revising a simple evaluation form?

But someone named Hawthorne had other ideas. If I asked my readers to tally violence, racial imbalance, or profanity, they'd be sure to find it. This was the dreaded "Hawthorne Effect"; shortly I began to wish I'd never heard of this person. For thirty days I shot from home to campus like a yo-yo. *How* I worded the questionnaire, the professor said, was every bit as important as the questions.

We agreed on a two-part form. Objectively, part 1 asks parent readers to tally what the author (not the reader) portrayed about race, handicaps, personal relationships, and world-life views. Subjectively, in part 2, readers express their reactions and quote from the books.

Finally! We had a working evaluation form, and twelve readers who were busier than two cats in a bathtub.

These readers knew the project wouldn't be simple, but they came aboard anyway. Give parents a curriculum project and get out of the way! A group of determined parents has more drive and creativity than most schools are brave enough to harness.

The parents (and two non-parents) who read these books are just like you. We love our kids and grandkids. As a group, we represent twenty-two children ages two to twenty-nine; four of the children are multi-racial or international adoptees (black Vietnamese, Indian, Korean). We have lots of teenagers!

Professionally, we work as writers, certified teachers, a bookstore owner, a stepparent, foster parents, a church publication executive committee member, an engineer, homemakers, a day-care operator, a seminary student, and one listee in *Who's Who in the World*.

Our spouses, who put up with this reading obsession for two years, work as a family physician, a school board member, a cement contractor, a full-time student, a plumber, a writer, a corporation vice-president, an attorney, and an interior decorator.

We don't claim to have turned our city upside down. Like other parents we come to parent-teacher meetings. We take our turns carpooling. We're up nights listening for the teenager's '68 Mustang to come home. We get the kids and ourselves to church. We're up to our elbows in the drug war. We pray.

A school maintenance worker caught the vision of this project and red-lined her prayer calendar for three years. Spiritual attacks were heavy and subtle; we found ourselves reaching into our spiritual "wardrobes" for every piece of armor described in Ephesians 6:10–18!

Ours is a university town. Most of us have been Iowans for ten years. But from our backgrounds you'll know we've been everywhere; this is not an insular club. People who participated with reading and analysis have lived in Virginia, New York, Kentucky, California, South

Dakota, Illinois, Montana, Pennsylvania, Texas, Morocco, the Philippines, Guam, and China. We know what "multi-cultural" means!

From our four reading projects in four cities, parents formally analyzed eighty-one books. I read them all, as well as hundreds of other

---

"Our poll of Iowa high school librarians shows no official parent input into library selection! "

---

books besides. Other parents did most of the reviews. It nearly killed me, but I kept my opinion out of their evaluations! I asked questions, but never challenged.

The parent as reader may be a new phenomenon. Our poll of Iowa high school librarians shows *no official parent input into library selection!* States that do have significant input from citizens concerning school curricula are often involved in flaming censorship litigation. The real issue in most of them is not whether citizens have the democratic right of comment, but whether educators in a well-oiled monopoly have more rights than the citizens who pay their salaries, and whether one pressure group gives a more fluent (or acceptable) argument than another.

Former Education Secretary Lauro Cavazos mourned the lack of pressure from parents. But while he begged school boards to explain *their* mission *to* the people, we say *parents should explain their mission to the school boards!*[3]

Barbara Walters' ABC Special, "Teaching Our Kids to Think," praised parental input. Walters was incredulous: the Japanese homemaker tutors her kids for another three to six hours after school![4] Walters should see grassroots action where parents on the front lines are involved in everything from drug skirmishes to student achievement. She should talk to the burgeoning number of parents whose kids learn math and English in one fourth the time in home schools. American parents are beginning to put their mouths where their hearts are.

Parents who now say *no* to drugs, tobacco, and child abuse are beginning to say *no* to increasing distortions of U.S. and world history and to a morally lopsided curriculum.

Do We Want Censorship—or Diversity?

But the main thrust of this study is not to say *no*. It is *not* to censor books. Check the curriculum challenges in chapter 5. Most parents read one book, then challenge. Or they leaf through their kids' homework, talk to a few parents, then march to the school board. Researching whole curricula and making recommendations for *diversity* is the key.

The 1987 Alabama secular humanism case was wildly distorted in the press. Few know that Judge Brevard Hand based his judgment on an indisputable base of objectively researched textbooks before he pronounced Alabama texts a violation of the First Amendment in their promotion of *one religion*: secular humanism.

Challenging a single book doesn't win schools back to balance and true diversity. Instead, it creates division. Parents who want their kids to read the truth should cry "diversity!" And they should see that this diversity includes the facts and values they're trying to teach their kids at home. It's the only winnable war, and the only constitutional one.

It's time to use our own "critical thinking" to put John Dewey in his place. This critical thinking guru and the "father of modern education" said there's no God and we must "re-think" Western culture. Essentially, his philosophy has excluded others from today's elementary and secondary education.

Parents' critical thinking based on whole truth stimulated a series of Congressional hearings from Seattle to Orlando. Parents testified not in favor of censorship, but to challenge a system of emotional and mental abuse of school children who are subtly denied a fair menu of thought. Testifying parents largely agreed: A handful of educators used a narrow, non-diverse curriculum to reshape the values of millions of children.[5]

It's diversity we're promoting. If you don't agree with our twelve reading parents, evaluate your own libraries (see chapter 6). We've done the hard work. It took us two years to refine an objective measuring system. With this tool kit, you can do a valid sampling of teen fiction in your school library in three months. This book shows you how.

2

How Do Books Get In the Library?

A insworth Spofford didn't worry about which books to buy. Friends brought him sacks full. He never turned down a book. When he ran out of shelves, he stacked them on the floor. When he ran out of floor, he had a unique solution: he became Librarian of Congress. In 1864 he bought two of every copyrighted book.

Today's Library of Congress has three huge buildings full of books. That's because it's the only library that can buy everything. Everyone else has to decide which books to buy and which to reject.

The two main restraints? Space and money. Spofford's only problem was *where* to put books. Today's librarian decides *which* books. This adds up to millions of mini decisions—someone must decide which books you'll see and which ones you'll never hear about.

If you saw your librarian at five o'clock last Friday you've guessed what this pressure is like, especially if his community doesn't like all his decisions.

Books may gain sacred status once they're stocked, but they don't leap on the shelves in the middle of the night, multiplying in dark corners. Someone—a real, live, vulnerable person or committee—decides which books of those Library of Congress millions go into your town or school. One midwestern city librarian says she "weeds" her collection carefully. She likes to "reflect her community" in her selection. "(My city) is a tad more erudite than some public libraries," she asserts. Somewhere in America now, there is a librarian who's thinking "erudite"—and her library is going to be different, perhaps more diverse, from yours or mine.

Your librarian can't buy every book, and she can't read all the books she buys. A mighty array of professionals from publisher to reviewer helps her decide which books rate shelf space.

The Process from Author to Teen

Let's take it direct from the author: the first to read her book is the publisher. If you're an author who wants wide readership for your teenage novel, start with one of the big publishers like Atheneum or Macmillan. They're the ones whose books get reviewed. And it's reviewed books that make it to your library and chain bookstores.

Pick a Popular Publisher

Big-company editors select from thousands of manuscripts yearly—mostly from agented writers. These editors have do's and don'ts. Lots of "do's" to new age, adventure, romance, drama. Some for gay/lesbian, and western. The don'ts? No tritely written, please. Only one company nixed excessive sex, violence, horror.

More and more editors, English teachers, librarians, and reviewers are female. Of the twelve large teen-fiction publishers in the 1990 *Writer's Market,* two-thirds of the editors making those teen fiction decisions are female.[1] Ninety percent of all librarians are female. Sixty-five percent of all secondary English teachers are female. And thus the reviewers, most of whom are teachers reviewing part-time—are mostly female. When we checked three libraries this year we found two of them stocking 90 percent female authors on our random-selection list. *Might it help to be female if you want your "young adult" novel on public shelves?*

And it certainly helps to have a book that will sell. The bottom line is profit. If you want publishers to change political or philosophical direction, you'll have to convince them they won't lose their shirts while they're aiding a cause. Obviously they study what sells. They read the bottom line in their marketing division. They talk to book distributors after school book fairs. They ask, "What did the kids pick?" Then they produce more. They ask, "What authors are favorites? Which authors get mail?" Those contracts get renewed.

From Publisher to Reviewer

If you're one of those tiny few whose teen-fiction book makes it to pre-publication, your bound, unpublished manuscript is whisked to a few hundred full-time, and hundreds of part-time reviewers. Your book is then reduced to a twenty-five to three hundred word review, and back it funnels to the major reviewing publications (like *School Library Journal, Booklist, Publishers Weekly, VOYA*). Monthly, quarterly, and yearly reviews then pop up via subscription in your town or school library.

> *"The bottom line is profit. If you want publishers to change political or philosophical direction, you'll have to convince them they won't lose their shirts while they're aiding a cause."*

The goal for every publishing company is to get at least two favorable reviews for each book they sell: this gives it the ring of professionalism and practically guarantees its presence in a library. Two reviews is also a safety-net for librarians—for such times when book challengers darken the door.

But librarians can't read every review! Just our yearly five top teen fiction lists produce 150 reviews as the cream-of-the crop of thousands. And this doesn't account for every teen-fiction review service or the non-fiction or reference books!

Since 1876, groups like the American Library Association have jumped in to help. *For the secondary school librarian alone* there are twenty-four review services listed in Nilsen and Donelson's library science text. Reading the list itself requires some time!

- *Alan Review*. National Council of Teachers of English. Young adult literature only. Reviews and articles.

- *Book Bait.* American Library Association. Help with adult books popular with young people. "Bridges the gap" between young adult and adult novels.

- *Booklist.* American Library Association. Reviews in twenty to three hundred words. Reviews mean recommended purchase. Teen section for high-interest, easy reading. Spring issue has "Best Books for Young Adults" list.

- *Books for the Teen Age.* Office of Young Adult Services, New York Public Library. Titles "tested and tried" with teen readers.

- *Books for You.* National Council of Teachers of English. List for Senior High Students. Fourteen hundred books reviewed by subject. "Frank or offensive" language noted. New editions every six or seven years. Classics and new books.

- *Bulletin of the Center for Children's Books.* University of Chicago Graduate Library School, University of Chicago Press. Includes both recommended and not recommended titles. Consistency of reviews under the editorship of a single individual.

- *Children's Literature in Education.* Joint work of United Kingdom and U. S. International Quarterly. "Substantive analysis rather than . . . quick once-overs." Young adult authors reviewed.

- *English Journal.* National Council of Teachers of English. "Aimed at high school English teachers." Yearly Young Adult Book Poll from University of Iowa.

- *High Interest-Easy Reading for Junior and Senior High Students.* National Council of Teachers of English. For "reluctant young adult readers" instead of parents or teachers. "High interest, easy reading, literary quality."

- *Horn Book Magazine.* Boston. Since 1924. Reviews of two-hundred words of both adult and young adult books. Aims for popular appeal first, literary quality second.

- *Interracial Books for Children Bulletin.* Council on Interracial Books for Children, New York. Social issues and their treatment in current fiction, non-fiction, and curriculum.

- *Journal of Reading.* International Reading Association, Newark, Del. Audience: high school reading teachers. The teaching of reading. Also young adult book reviews.

- *Junior High School Library Catalog.* H. W. Wilson Company, New York. Book collection for junior high libraries. Reference tool with books in Dewey Decimal. "Outstanding reference tool for junior high school librarians."

- *Kirkus Reviews.* Kirkus Service, New York. Expensive, but up to date. Two hundred word reviews, with section for young adult books.

- *Kliatt Paperback Book Guide.* Newton, Mass. Reviews all paperbacks recommended for twelve to nineteen-year-olds. Coded for use for advanced, general readers, junior high, low reading ability, and emotionally mature readers who can handle "explicit sex, excessive violence and/or obscenity."

- *New York Times Book Review. New York Times,* New York. Fall and spring issues lean heavily towards children's books, including their list of "best books."

- *Reading Ladders for Human Relations.* American Council on Education and National Council of Teachers of English. Five categories: "Growing into Self, Relating to Wide Individual Differences, Interacting in Groups, Appreciating Different Cultures, Coping in a Changing World."

- *School Library Journal.* R. R. Bowker Company, New York. "Most comprehensive." Reviews both recommended and not recommended. Panel of four hundred librarians are sent novels "particularly appropriate to their interests and backgrounds." Includes starred reviews.

- *Senior High School Library Catalog.* H. W. Wilson Co., New York. (See *Junior High Catalog.*)

- *Top of the News.* Joint publication of Association for Library Service to Children and the Young Adult Services Division of the American Library Association, Chicago. Feature articles and reviews of professional publications.

- *Voice of Youth Advocates (VOYA).* Alabama. One of its aims: "To change the traditional linking of young adult services with children's librarianship and shift the focus to its connection with adult services." Articles give views "not commonly considered." Books reviewed on "PQ" system: 5P, 5Q review means tops in popularity and literary merit.

- *Wilson Library Bulletin.* H. W. Wilson Co., New York. Reviews current books and other media for young adults. Focus is "much broader than young adult librarianship."[2]

Not included in the 1985 Nilsen/Donelson book is *Parents' Choice* of Waban, Massachusetts. This review service for younger parents also offers early teen fiction. It has a hopeful come-on: "All material concerning the imaginative life of the child." Barbara Bush is on the board. So is Kitty Dukakis. They claim to "separate the good from the not-so-good and make it easy for you to choose only the best for your kids."

School Lists of "Favorites"

In addition to these professional helps, each school makes its own teen-favorite list. That way, kids can see whether they are normal readers or out in left field somewhere. Besides these local lists there are state favorites (Iowa Teen Award), national pop lists, and teacher persuasion.

If librarians with Steven King fever also hype their student body with King mania via reading contests, you can be sure the "safe to read King" climate will produce more readership, thus more publishing— sales—profit. If Steinbeck's *Grapes of Wrath* is not pushed by librarians and teachers, there's a very real possibility it will "die out," as one fearful commentator prophesied.

The Library Selections

As the trend trickles down the line—from publisher to reviewer to librarian to student—momentum builds and values change. If it's okay to talk about condoms in fiction now, you can be sure (as I heard from a media specialist in his workshop) that a part-time teacher-reviewer will put in his 1990 review, "After Dick and Jane have safe sex" as a kind of afterthought. If that comment slips quietly by, bolder ones follow. Parents don't see these reviews; they're at the library, but usually not on the shelves.

On most library office shelves is *Books for You:* It's a hefty tome reviewing literature from classics to modern teenage novels. Because the review is only published every five to seven years, some of its back issues are more likely to include a racially balanced selection. More black authors were being published in the sixties and seventies, "when children's book publishers were opening up to blacks," says John Steptoe, black author/illustrator.[3]

In fact, you might find widely different "young adult" library promotionals in any given region of the country. But every school listens to National Council of Teachers of English or American Library Association. These and *School Library Journal* are welcome guests wherever they go.

But are reviewers reliable? Nilsen says *Books for You* warns of "frank or offensive language." Does it? *Books for You* notes *Vision Quest's* live-in girlfriend,[4] but gives mute go-ahead to an explicit sex melee with three brothers and their one-night girlfriends in *Center Line.*[5]

I've read hundreds of these quickie one-paragraph reviews. They're out to make the book look good. The best is canonized; the rest, euphemized. You learn to read between the lines when you see a smoothie like this: "This is a realistic story of personal growth." We saw one half-hearted effort to expose a story's vitals with University of Iowa's Young Adult Poll. The reviewer said her book was "captivating" and "exciting," while noting "the killing and gore require a strong stomach."

Longer reviews might concede that a story courts parent wrath. That's the way reviewers let the librarian know the book is morally bankrupt.

It's hard enough to decipher positively-worded reviews. Librarians also have to contend with hard-sell ads. Side by side with Marion Bauer's recent *Top of the News* anti-censorship article was a children's

---

"I've read hundreds of these quickie one-paragraph reviews. They're out to make the book look good. The best is canonized; the rest, euphemized."

---

book ad from a major publisher. *Booklist* ran a similar ad for librarians while promoting their "Best Books for Young Adults" (March 15, 1988—used as one of our lists for this project). There's an Atheneum ad for *The Return*, by Sonia Levitin, and *Sons from Afar* by Cynthia Voigt (both in our reading project). If the librarian flips to *School Library*

Journal and sees the same book ad, it isn't long before name recognition vies for judgment.

Kids don't have to worry about hard-sell ads in librarians' reviews, but they do have to face the school library's own soft-sell. If a librarian sees teenagers devouring one author or subject, he'll capitalize with posters like: "What to read when you've read Ray Bradbury (or Judy Blume or Isaac Asimov)." Thus a teenager fascinated with biking or whales or suicide or science fiction doesn't have to look far for the next novel or documentary: These pop-reader lists beat him to the card catalog.

Which teen-fiction reviews does your library use? Our poll of fifty randomly selected Iowa high school librarians confirmed our hunch: The five promotional lists used in our parent project rank highest in Iowa library purchase decisions.

The University of Northern Iowa youth librarian, Assistant Professor Lucille Lettow, and one of the University of Northern Iowa's English professors agreed with the Iowa ranking and said all but the local Iowa Teen Award are widely used favorites nationally. VOYA squeaked out as a close sixth. Though not every state uses the supposedly local Iowa Teen Award, any ten sample lists of "best-read" teen fiction will show you Teen Award's books plus all of our forty-five. *You'll see the same books over and over.*

The "Cream of the Crop" Our 1988 List of Forty-Five Titles

What follows is the "best list" for one year: 1988. This random selection of forty-five from a cream-of-the-crop list of 150 is what our twelve parents read and carefully analyzed. They're representative of the young adult novels promoted for eleven to eighteen-year-olds. Here are the word-for-word reviews including errors as published in national promotional lists.

I. Best Books for Young Adults, 1987 (American Library Association, published in *Booklist,* March 15, 1988)

"This annual list of books compiled by a committee of the Young Adult Services Division of the American Library Association consists of 81 titles appropriate for young adults ages 12 to 18. They were selected on the basis of each book's proven or potential appeal and worth to young adult readers, and they span a wide variety of subjects for different reading tastes as well as a broad range of reading levels."[6]

- *The Crossing,* by Gary Paulsen (Watts/Orchard/Richard Jackson). "An alcoholic army sergeant and a homeless Mexican orphan come together in an unlikely friendship."

- *The Dark City,* by Max Allan Collins (Bantam). "After leaving Chicago, legendary gangbuster Eliot Ness goes to Cleveland to clean up a corrupt police force."

- *Denny's Tapes,* by Carolyn Meyer (Macmillan/Margaret K. McElderry). "Ejected by his stepfather, Dennis goes across country in search of his real father, detouring to visit both his grandmothers, from whom he learns about his biracial heritage."

- *Ellen Foster,* by Kaye Gibbons (Algonquin). "After her mother's untimely death, young Ellen must survive despite her abusive father and other relatives who want no part of her, in a story filled with tears—and laughter too."

- *The Goats,* by Brock Cole (Farrar). "Stripped naked by fellow campers and left on a deserted island, social misfits Laura and Howie survive humiliation, natural dangers—and each other."

- *I Remember Valentine,* by Liz Hamlin (Dutton). "A seriocomic view of the Depression through the eyes of an 11-year-old girl who learns about four-letter words and sex when she moves next door to the infamous Hart family."

- *Isaac Campion,* by Jannie Howker (Greenwillow). "The death of his older brother forces young Isaac to assume the entire burden of working on his vicious father's horse farm in turn-of-the-century England."

- *Jimmy D., Sidewinder, and Me,* by Otto R. Salassi (Greenwillow). "In jail, 15-year-old Dumas Monk is writing—on the judge's orders—the story of how he became a pool hustler and a murderer."

- *Many Waters,* by Madeleine L'Engle (Farrar). "Intruding in their father's lab, twins Sandy and Dennys are flung across time to a desert where Noah's family lives among mythical creatures."

- *Princess Ashley,* by Richard Peck (Delacorte, distributed by Double-day). "New girl Chelsea must decide what price she is willing to pay to win popular Ashley Packard's acceptance."

- *Seventh Son,* by Orson Scott Card (Tor, distributed by St. Martin's). "Alvin, born seventh son of a seventh son, is destined for greatness, but something evil is trying to keep him from growing up."

- *Sons from Afar,* by Cynthia Voigt (Atheneum). "Dicey's brothers, on the brink of growing up, search for the father who deserted them as infants—and find unforeseen truths."

- *Through the Hidden Door,* by Rosemary Wells (Dial, distributed by Dutton). "A bullied prep school student discovers his inner strengths as he helps the school misfit excavate a mysterious ruin."

- *Waiting for the Rain,* by Sheila Gordon (Watts/Orchard/Richard Jackson). "On a South African farm, Tengo, black, and Frikkie, white, forge a friendship that is later challenged by the injustices of apartheid."

- *What I Did for Roman,* by Pam Conrad (Harper). "Vulnerable Darcie becomes involved with a handsome, disturbed young man while working at the zoo."

- *What Niall Saw,* by Brian Cullen (St. Martin's). "The misspelled fragments in a seven-year-old Irish boy's diary after the Bomb offers a chilling testament to the end of the world."[7]

II. "Books for Children and Young Adults" and Adult Books for Young Adults (*School Library Journal,* December, 1987)

This list "includes titles for all ages—in fiction and non-fiction." The total list of 57 recommended titles is the "best of the more than 2700 books reviewed this year (1987)." Literature "took a quality leap this year . . . and is respectful of the capacity for intellectual and emotional growth of the young adult audience." [8]

- *M. E. and Morton,* by Sylvia Cassedy (Crowell). Grades 5-8. "A peculiar and bossy new girl dramatically changes the lives of a lonely, imaginative child and her older, retarded brother. The texture of the plot and the lovingly wrought, achingly real characterizations make this novel one to linger over and share."

- *The Return,* by Sonia Levitin (Atheneum). Grade 7 and up. "An absorbing survival adventure, based on 'Operation Moses,' about young participants in a secret airlift that flew hundreds of Falasha Jews from Ethiopia to Israel. A modern day exodus that explores prejudice, tolerance, and compassion."

- *After the Rain,* by Norma Fox Mazer (Morrow). Grade 6 and up. "A coming of age story in which a teenage girl and her family coalesce around the girl's cantankerous grandfather in the last months of his life. Mazer's uncomplicated prose showcases a rainbow of memorable characters."

- *The Year Without Michael,* by Susan Beth Pfeffer (Bantam). Grades 9–12. "About to enter high school, Michael disappears. Pfeffer focuses on the course of his family's reactions and their raw emotions as they interact with each other. Taut structure, sound characterization, and honest dialogue make the months of uncertainty, fear, and anger a year to remember."

- *The Tricksters,* by Margaret Mahy (McElderry Books, Macmillan). Grade 9 and up. "Family tensions explode when the chicanery of three handsome and mysterious visitors precipitate the unwelcomed revelation of domestic secrets. Mahy's intricate and perceptive story is masterful in its complexities, subtleties, and development of relationships."[9]

The following are "Best Adult Books for Young Adults," selected by the Houston area Adult Books for Young Adults committee from SLJ's reviews between October, 1986 and November, 1987.

"Selecting books that would add currency and depth . . . as well as books that would be popular."

- *Bobby Rex's Greatest Hit,* by Marianne Gingher (Atheneum). "A novel detailing how Pally Thompson, heroine of Bobby Rex's greatest hit song, deals with her life after the song's release. The characters are created lovingly, and events are in turn hilarious and tragic. Adolescents will recognize their own feelings and hopes in Pally's."

- *If I Were You,* by Joan Aiken (Doubleday). "A charming story of exchanged identities whose archetypal characters examine the differences between appearance and reality. A light romance which will appeal to readers across the generations."

- *Maus: A Survivor's Tale,* by Art Spiegelman (Pantheon). "Told with chilling realism in an unusual comic book format, this is more than a tale of surviving the Holocaust. It relates events which young adults must confront, and their interest is sure to be caught by the skillful graphics and suspenseful unfolding of the story."

- *Red Storm Rising,* by Tom Clancy (Putnam). "A fast-paced, vivid scenario of nuclear holocaust, involving confrontation between two superpowers. The complex characters reveal a new vision of war. Outstanding."[10]

III. *Iowa Teen Award 1987–88 Masterlist* (Iowa Educational Media Association)

1989 IEMA President Mary Knox (librarian at Parkview Jr. High, Ankeny, Iowa), says books on the Masterlist have to be published within the three years previous to the list. They can't be in a series, and they have to have been reviewed. Up to thirty specialists from Iowa rate them according to a rating chart. Forty books make the next list, from which students choose fifteen. The purpose of the Masterlist: "to encourage students to read more and better books; to discriminate in choosing worthwhile books; to provide an avenue for positive dialogue between teachers, parents, and students about books and authors; to give recognition to those who write books for early teens."[11] The list gave no book descriptions.

- *Abby, My Love,* by Hadley Irwin (Atheneum).
- *Buddies,* by Barbara Park (Knopf).
- *The Changeover,* by Margaret Mahy (Atheneum/Scholastic).
- *Corky and The Brothers Cool,* by P. J. Petersen (Delacorte).
- *Strictly for Laughs,* by Ellen Conford (Pacer/Putnam).
- *When The Phone Rang,* by Harry Mazer (Scholastic).

IV. "University of Iowa's Books for Young Adults Poll" (*English Journal,* January, 1988)

Letters to all major publishers provided a base of four hundred newly published books. Four hundred and fifty young people from individualized reading courses in southeastern Iowa then selected twenty-five fiction and non-fiction books. They chose books for "initial appeal" and "enjoyment." Published annually in the *Journal*, this is not a regional project, but a national list.

- *Circus Day,* by Caroline Crane (Dodd, Mead). "Kate Armstrong knows she talks too much. As she and her two young children leave a circus gala at a shopping mall, Kate strikes up a conversation with a man in the parking lot, and she unwisely reveals to him that her husband is away on a business trip. Kate and her children are taken hostage by the man and his accomplice who have robbed a bank and need transportation. Kate is certain that once they reach their destination she and her children will be killed. "I enjoyed the way the author realistically created the kidnapping situation and displayed the emotions of the family."

- *Don't Blame the Music,* by Caroline Cooney (Putnam). "Within the first few weeks of her senior year, Susan must face the traumatic return of her older sister, Ashley, a hostile hard rocker drowning in self-hatred. As music editor of the yearbook, Susan befriends a new set of classmates, non-conformists who provide her with insight into Ashley's troubling behavior. Despite her anger over Ashley's embarrassing and often violent outbursts, Susan remains loyal to her sister, an important step toward maturity."

- *Getting Even,* by Susan Beth Pfeffer (Pacer/Putnam). "After eight weeks as a summer intern at glamorous *Image* magazine, Annie Powell dreads leaving New York City and returning to Boston for her senior year in high school. Annie becomes angry and resentful when she learns she has not been selected feature editor of the school newspaper. Balancing a boyfriend, a new public relations job, and school is Annie's way of getting even with those who underrated her talent. But can she handle the stress?" A sixteen-year-old reader recommends this "to people in high school who are trying to figure out where they fit into the world."

- *Halfback Tough,* by Thomas J. Dygard (Morrow). "Joe Atkins enrolls at Graham High and proves himself an excellent halfback and a good student. Joe likes the notoriety accompanying success but fears that his poor school record and troublemaking friends from his previous school will pursue him. Before a hard-fought game with the best team in the conference, Coach Steel surprises Joe, telling him that he is aware of Joe's troubled past but has not said anything because he wants him to prove he can succeed in this new school. 'It's reality,' one reader said. Another responded, 'I related—I just came to this school and went through similar stuff.'"

- *IT,* by Stephen King (Viking). "In 1957 a child disappears down a storm drain in a small town called Derry. The following summer five boys and a girl, 'the losers,' desperately band together to fight an unspeakable horror. They grow up and forget the evil which haunted their childhood. Twenty-seven years later each of them receives a phone call. One commits suicide; the others return to Derry and reunite to face a dimly remembered terror. Readers found it 'intriguing,' 'captivating,' 'exciting,' but also noted that the killing and gore required 'a strong stomach.'"

- *Loydene in Love,* by Lael Littke (Harcourt Brace Jovanovich). "Loydene's grandmother tells her that the sooner a girl finds a guy to marry and settles down to raise a family, the happier she will be. Loydene isn't so sure she believes that anymore, especially when she goes to Los Angeles to visit her friend, Shanny. Shanny introduces Loydene to an exciting guy named Jakey and helps Loydene get a job acting in a TV commercial. But, Loydene feels strong ties to her home in Wolf Creek and her sturdy, reliable high school sweetheart, nicknamed 'U-haul.' 'I like the theme of a small-town girl visiting a big city where she meets a fast-paced guy and is torn between him and her sweetheart at home.'"[12]

V. "Young Adult Editors' Choice," (National Council of Teachers of English, published in *Booklist,* January 15, 1988)

"From the books published in 1987, the . . . titles have been selected as 'top choices' . . . by the *Booklist* Books for Young Adults staff—editor, Sally Estes. Although the emphasis is on adult titles, some outstanding young adult books with appeal for older teenagers are included."[13]

- *Eyes of the Dragon,* by Stephen King (Viking). "In a charming fairy tale of good versus evil that comes complete with poisonous brews, secret passages, and malevolent sorcerers, a magician schemes to do a well-loved prince out of his royal inheritance."

- *Good-Bye and Keep Cold,* by Jenny Davis (Watts/Orchard/Richard Jackson). "'I am resting from my childhood,' explains Edda Combs as she looks back on her life in rural Kentucky after her father died in a strip-mining accident when she was a child and her mother tentatively took up with the man responsible."

- *Greencastle,* by Lloyd Kropp (Freundlich/Scribner). "An outsider at school, 16-year-old Roger Cornell thinks life is good because two friends share his interests, but when he tries to befriend a mysterious, undefinable boy-genius, Roger discovers a hidden, darker world."

- *Invincible Summer,* by Jean Ferris (Farrar). "Seventeen-year-old Robin, recently diagnosed as having cancer, learns about love and loss from Rick, funny, wise, and dying of leukemia."

- *I Only Made Up the Roses,* by Barbara Ann Porte (Greenwillow). "A keen observer of those around her, Cydra stitches a strong patchwork of familial devotion, introducing herself and her nurturing interracial family, in a novel filled with wit, warmth, and poignancy."

- *Permanent Connections,* by Sue Ellen Bridgers (Harper). "Restive, hostile, and citywise, Rob is forced to move in with some relatives in rural North Carolina, where he gradually begins to make sense of his life and reconnect with his family."

- *Rich in Love,* by Josephine Humphreys (Viking). "Firmly rooted in her South Carolina home, 17-year-old Lucille remains a strong center for her troubled parents and her beautiful, pregnant older sister, as Lucille herself finds passion and self-acceptance."

- *The River in Winter,* by David Small (Norton). "After assaulting his sadistic stepfather and stealing his gun, an angry teenager escapes to try to find a modicum of happiness with his lonely grandfather."[14]

What's Wrong with This Picture?

In these 45 reviews, as in the 150 original reviews, *there are no Christian publishers!* Why do reviewers responsible to all the public school and city libraries in the United States review so few Christian books that none showed up in the "best" lists?

What happened between the publisher and the reviewer? We know there are adult novels, teen novels, and children's books with Christian themes which are selling in the hundreds of thousands—even millions. Where are they?

Christian Publishers in a Secular World

Kathy Jacobs of Crossway Books says they've plowed tough ground in the secular world, including reviews in *Booklist,* with Steven Lawhead's popular *Pendragon Cycle.* Also widely read by older teens are Frank Peretti's *This Present Darkness* and *Piercing the Darkness,* which have sold over 2.5 million copies. After five years of sales Peretti's explosive novels are finally boiling the waters in secular newspapers (except the *New York Times* best-seller list), and bringing phone calls from librarians whose young patrons want autobiographical material for book reports. VOYA also reviews Crossway's teen fiction, but they're not always complimentary. "It's generally correct that (your major reviewers) don't review us. So our goal is just to target those who consistently show our books for what they are—literarily and morally excellent," Jacobs states.

Jacobs sends press releases and galley copies to hundreds of libraries and reviewing services, but admits the job could be done more thoroughly. "What's needed," she says, "is for a few Christian publishers to sit down with reviewers and librarians and tell them what Christian publishing is all about."[15]

Jeanie Mikkelson of Bethany House is confident that since *Publishers Weekly* is responding more favorably to America's clamor for more religious books, her company's books will now get reviewed. And she thinks it would be a positive move for *PW* and other secular magazines to publish Christian best-seller lists *in combination* with secular lists.

Bethany House has sold 7.5 million of the widely popular Janette Oke pioneer-theme books for ages ten through adult. Their Cedar River Daydreams novels for ten to fifteen-year-olds, which compete favorably with the secular Sweet Valley High series, have sold 330,000. With such controversial themes as date rape, child abuse, teen suicide, the environment, and rebellion, Daydream's same teenagers handle a new problem with each novel. Bethany House publishes four Daydreams books per year, and author Judy Baer receives twenty to thirty letters a week from readers. "In fifteen novels these kids are going to get a life-view that can really help them," says Mikkelson.[16]

Bias in Reviews and Promotions

So why aren't they stocked? No reviews, no sales. And until librarians get the word from patrons that it's the favorable climate to stock Christian books, you probably won't find a Christian reviewing service in your library.

"Why do reviewers responsible to all the public school and city libraries in the United States review so few Christian books that none showed up in the 'best' lists?"

Because shooting for literary balance earns the "censorship" or "violation of separation of church and state" label, fewer and fewer librarians and reviewers are willing to include current novels with heroes who are in open and honest relationship with God. Bryce Christensen regrets the official wisdom that allows only books of religious "description" (not devotional) in the public school library: "Poets and novelists may describe prayer . . . but may not actually pray."[17]

Maybe the *New York Times* isn't afraid of "separation of church and state," but something made them leave out Francis Schaeffer's *Christian Manifesto,* which sold over 330,000 in fifteen months. On their list several times was Jack Henry Abbot's *In the Belly of the Beast,* which sold 150,000 copies in ten months.[18]

Nor did the *New York Times* acknowledge best-seller Frank Peretti's powerfully Christian *This Present Darkness* (Crossway Books, 1986). This book sold nearly a million copies before some libraries knew it existed. *Library Journal* reviews (not favorably) Peretti's 1989 sequel *Piercing the Darkness* with the annotation: "for public libraries" (Did you know professional reviewers slate some books "for church libraries"?). How will public school librarians know about these quality books, when Christian novels don't make it to the professional lists or the *New York Times* best-seller roll call?

Secular bookstores are not accurate barometers for Christian bookselling or library purchase either. Cal Thomas in *Book Burning* says that "according to Christian publisher Bruce Barbour of Fleming H. Revell Company, Brentano's and many other major bookstores show little interest in new Christian titles, no matter how well they are selling."[19]

Thomas notes that in the B. Dalton bookstore in Lynchburg, Virginia, "The 'Religion and Inspirational' section, in the rear of the store by the emergency exit and the toilet, consists of twenty-five titles, including everything from Jerry Falwell . . . to *Shamanism: Archaic Techniques of Ecstasy.*"[20]

Has this situation improved since Thomas' scouting mission of 1983? One of our readers found only twenty-four inches of "religious" books in a major bookstore in downtown Washington, D.C. in 1989, as well as in his hometown book store. And, yes, it was back in the corner by the exit sign.

Big chain bookstores hold book fairs in local schools. What they sell reflects what kids pick. But the kids don't have a full deck to deal from.

The end result of this less-than-perfect reviewing and weeding is what one California librarian calls "a move from stimulating classics to titillating new fiction."

"I never realized until I turned nineteen," said a young man from Wisconsin, "that teen fiction in my high school gave me lots of smut and garbage. My mind was a computer then, taking it all in." After spending a year on drugs, this former high school student is taking a new look at his life.

Kathleen Baxter, coordinator of children's services at Anoka County Library in Minnesota in 1985, notes her surprise at becoming so liberal she's "closed her mind." She's afraid she has "become as prejudiced as those people whose conservative prejudices I deplore."[21]

Lamenting the barren wasteland of "good" Christian books, she explains why she doesn't buy many: "Christian publishers were choosing substandard authors and illustrators, bindings, paper, to proselytize beliefs which are important to them."[22]

She wonders if most reviewers give Christian books the overly harsh scrutiny she was beginning to employ. Writing to school librarians, she says: ". . . religion in children's books seems to be a persona non grata to most reviewers. . . . if the protagonist of a children's story is religious, then the chances of that story getting a good review are seriously diminished."[23]

Day-care operator Staci Charles of Hiawatha, Kansas, agrees. A former public school teacher, Charles bemoans the fact that good Christian books by authors like Steven Lawhead, Bodie Thoene, and Frank Peretti, which often outsell their secular counterparts ". . . do not appear in major book review magazines or on the 'bestseller' lists. In fact, no

---

"The pervasive mindset among teachers of library science and young adult literature is that minorities, women, and the handicapped who cry for change have pure motives. Those who ask for historical accuracy in religion, and who want their Christian voice added to the marketplace, are censors of the worst kind."

Christian bookstores are polled for these charts."[24] "If we are really going to 'separate church and state,' then we need to treat books containing atheist or agnostic statements with the same segregation that Christian books have received."[25]

Censorship

The pervasive mindset among teachers of library science and young adult literature is that minorities, women, and handicaps who cry for change have pure motives. Those who ask for historical accuracy in religion, and who want their Christian voice added to the marketplace, are censors of the worst kind.

Nilsen and Donelson's college text, *Literature for Today's Young Adults,* implies that the reviewing service *Interracial Books for Children Bulletin* is only a mild censorship attempt. This Bulletin promotes racially balanced books which don't "stereotype" ethnic groups. But because the Texas-based Gablers make the same point with "stereotyped" religious points of view, Nilsen gives them top-of-the-line censorship status.

But to their credit, librarians also accuse themselves of censorship. Marion Dane Bauer, in Fall, 1984 *Top of the News,* sympathizes with librarians who confront parent censors. But she knows librarians censor, too. Once we get started on that, she wonders: "Where do we begin?" or more importantly "Where do we end?"[26]

(Bauer's novel *On My Honor*—about the negligent drowning of a twelve-year-old—was under fire after one city gave it district-wide fourth-grade assignment status. Parents objected to its "hopeless" treatment of life after death, but jumped on the tiny amount of profanity as the safest target. Newspaper accounts and board meeting censorship made the parents look ridiculous and the person-centered theme was never confronted.)

These reviewers and librarians use *Information Power,* a short library science textbook, so they know *all* subjects should "balance" library selection. Aside from the controversial "A person's right to use a library should not be denied . . . because of . . . age," these *Information Power* guidelines have the right stuff. Now all we have to do is *use* them! Christian books and other "controversial" subjects *belong* to the public which demands balanced fare.[27]

Now for the hard question: What if a lone librarian reads *Information Power* and decides to follow its blueprint for diversity? What if he's brave enough to try stocking teen fiction with Christian themes? The chances of his finding updated, popular Christian books in the reviews are slim. For three years I've read *Booklist, VOYA,* Children's Edition of *Publishers Weekly, School Library Journal, Horn Book* and others. Here are the types of *Christian books* most likely to make the reviewing stand:

- Books for younger kids (under twelve)—but mostly from secular publishers.

- Books over thirty years old.

- Books about famous Bible stories, but not about present-day Christians.

- Non-fiction such as autobiography.

- Minute number of titles from select Christian publishers (very few; no one seems to know how they're picked.)

Subjective Selection

How does one elementary school librarian handle this problem? "I just buy the Janette Oke books because they're good books," says a Midwestern librarian who wishes to remain anonymous. "I didn't find them in the reviews. I just knew about them," she said. And her school kids? They gobble them up. But this librarian is unusual. If you want to shoot a conversation dead, and raise tension to Excedrin levels, ask a school librarian why he doesn't diversify his library with Christian books.

Though elementary schools don't face the crushing rate of profanity and premarital sexual activity of the high-school books, increasingly librarians are faced with "mature themes" targeted for fifth through eighth, or middle schools. If middle-school librarians choose only from censored secular lists, they may have to resort to reading every single book they bring through the front door of the school.

The library staff of Princeton Elementary School District No. 115, Princeton, Illinois, pick their books carefully: It's worth our study, because pre-teens want to read very grown-up "teen" novels.

Almost every year, district librarian Connie Espel and the four building's library "clerks" go to Follett Library Book Company (Crystal Lake, Illinois). They cull books all day before they buy. And that's not all. The library staff also chooses books from:

- Teacher and student recommendations

- The classics list

- The Newbery Award and Honor Book List

- Outstanding Authors of the Twentieth Century List

- Titles suggested in subject-area textbooks

And they leaf through fiction from book company reps. Their goal: "To strive for the best books for each library building's collection and clientele."[28]

Is a city library vulnerable to lopsided stocks? I leafed through guidelines from Littleton, Colorado; Schenectady County, New York; and Kingsport, Tennessee, libraries. They all say about the same thing: Among the regulations is this heartening harbinger: they "consider the total needs of the community." One of these libraries says they'll choose fiction to "the extent of public interest in a given title, author, or genre."[29]

Would a librarian whose community is "forty-eight percent churched" stock the young adult section with forty-eight percent Christian themes? Would a community with seventy-five percent Jewish population stock seventy-five percent Jewish themes? Would a predominantly black neighborhood school library even have *access* to black-theme fiction? There seems to be a basic "stock" of "appropriately diverse and controversial" fiction which is only slightly varied from library to library.

First Amendment Issues

A fifth-grade teacher who took a tiny step towards diversity nearly took a big step out the door of his career. Ken Roberts of the Denver suburb of Westminster, Colorado put two overtly Christian books with 237 others on his classroom's "free reading" shelf. (It's standard in most classrooms: English teachers, junior high especially, build such "mini libraries" of their own paperbacks with revolving loans from the school library.)

Until two years ago, Roberts' class could pick and choose, reading on their own for fifteen minutes a day. Sometimes Roberts would read silently from his own personal Bible while kids sampled books which included media-sensationalized fiction which "conservative parents" want to censor: books like *Charlotte's Web, Tom Sawyer, The Wizard of Oz.*

After an angry parent complained about the Christian books, principal Kathleen Madigan ordered both Roberts' personal Bible and Christian stories removed. The case reached Federal Court, and in January 1989 the Judge ordered the Bible back on the shelf. *But the two Christian books were banned* "because children are impressionable," and "it would violate the Establishment Clause."[30] But no one banned Ken Roberts' classroom talks about Native American spirituality. The principal said "that was fine because the Indians prayed to a rainbow goddess and not to Jesus."[31] A federal appeals court on December 17, 1990 upheld the decision. The next step: The Supreme Court.[32]

Joan Podchernikoff, *USA Today* guest editorialist, lambastes the policy which put Judy Blume's *Deenie* in her kids' library. She said the book is "pornographic" and that petting, intercourse, and masturbation were "titillating." She and her husband weren't interested in "banning" books, only that the school library be "more accessible to parents."

But the point of her editorial—whether or not you agree with her reaction to Blume—underscores my point: Why are school officials like the principal's secretary in Podchernikoff's community *"screening books to make sure there was no reference to God?"* The principal said the secretary "should have caught these (pornographic) passages" while she was looking for the "God" references!

"So the school is engaging in censorship," says this mother of three. And this shows how far some schools and public libraries will go to "protect" the First Amendment![33]

> *"There seems to be a basic 'stock' of*
> *'appropriately diverse and controversial'*
> *fiction which is only slightly varied*
> *from library to library."*

In one small Iowa community, an elementary principal interpreted state "multi-cultural non-sexist" updates as directives to remove all fiction books showing mothers as traditional homemakers.

One Western librarian feared for her job: "Don't quote me," she said. "My religious views are in the minority." Censorship abounds, and it's not always by the "religious right."

Maybe it was fear that kept one librarian from stocking Eldridge Cleaver's *Soul on Fire.* Had the library balanced Cleaver's *Soul on Ice* with his later *Soul on Fire* before parents demanded its removal, the clash might have been averted. Cleaver's Christian conversion in *Fire* puts a different light on his radical *Ice.* And wouldn't it be fun to stock Charles Darwin's deathbed recant? In his waning years Darwin unraveled his evolution theories.

Likewise, if school librarians who face parental rage over occult teenage books would stock Satan-worship warnings like Mike Warnke's *The Satan Seller,* Tipper Gore's *Raising PG Kids in an X-Rated Society,* and Pat Pulling's *The Devil's Web,* students could read balance. When whole Truth and falsehood struggle, Truth wins: That's learning.

I've seen as many as eighty-five ghost-story, occult, and satanic books in a single junior-high library. But in most school libraries I've visited, overtly positive "personal-God-centered" fiction is only a tiny percentage of all fiction, if indeed there *is* any.

Library balance could have softened the Cleveland, Oklahoma challenge in 1988. Parents objected because blatantly satanic books lined the shelves; similar books on opposing views did not. This is *not* in keeping with the Library Bill of Rights:

> "Libraries should provide materials and information presenting all points of view on current and historical issues. Materials should not be proscribed or removed because of doctrinal disapproval."[34]

But note the carefully-chosen language of *Information Power*. The words "doctrinal" and "disapproval" are subjective. *Information Power* is loaded with other value words as well, like "good" and "cherished," "possessed of enormous variety and usefulness."[35] There's nothing wrong with value words—but *let's not pretend we're operating in a valueless vacuum.* Text writers, teachers, librarians, and parents come to their jobs with values. There's no such thing as robot decisions, no matter how lofty the guidelines.

Special Interest Groups

That tight bottleneck which chokes out good Christian fiction produces the inevitable lobbyists, or special interest groups, like Mel and Norma Gabler of Texas.

The Gablers are private citizen reviewers of textbooks; Michael Scott Cain calls them "professional censors."[36] Their special interest is the historical accuracy of subjects like patriotism and traditional values. In legal accord with the Texas system of citizen curriculum review, the Gablers simply put in their two-bits' worth along with everyone else, including the National Organization of Women. The Gablers have clout because they're deadly accurate and millions agree with them. And that makes some people furious enough to call them censors.

Shooting for balance of a different sort is the American Library Association's Gay and Lesbian Task Force. Apparently there weren't enough quality gay themes for ALA to recommend. So the task force got up an "Award for Exceptional Achievement," and its first winner gave us a book—"a loving depiction" about straights and gays, an "engaging, diverse group."[37] If ALA gave the award—they're going to recommend the book. Highly.

There would be more parent textbook review committees if we weren't afraid of hostile comments like the Kawaha County, West Virginia reports: "By September, the board knew it was outgunned. *It voted to have the books reviewed by a citizen's committee, an act comparable to letting an armed mortal enemy loose on prisoners of war.* The books were removed from the schools for a thirty-day examination period."[emphasis mine][38]

When Do Parents Get to Recommend?

Now it seems that everyone—including special interest groups like the Gablers and the American Library Association—is recommending books for your teens. Everyone but parents. Even *Parents' Choice* is the opinion of professional educators—not parents. *Parents' Choice* showed how they felt about parent input when they gave high ratings to TV's "Mighty Mouse." Even after thousands of angry parents flooded CBS with protests, *Parents' Choice* dismissed this "absurd flap" and called "Mighty Mouse" "the new darling among 1988 winners."[39] What did Mighty Mouse do on Saturday morning in full view of millions of children? Law-enforcement officers agree: He was sniffing cocaine.

Where Do Parents Fit In?

A poll of 50 Iowa high school librarians (with 27 responding) shows how they select books:[40]

Ways Librarians Select Books	Number of Schools
Librarian does all selecting	14
Librarian plus faculty	13
Librarian plus students	8
Librarian plus administration	2
Librarian plus school board	0
Librarian plus parents	0

There's a quick nod of approval from most school boards and administrations after the librarian turns in her purchase list. The librarian is trained to select; her choices usually go unchallenged until they're on the shelf and read by someone who wants them off.

Promotional Lists These Librarians Use	Number of Librarians
Iowa Teen Award	25
Booklist	22
School Library Journal	22
Best Books for Young Adults	19
U. of IA Poll (*English Journal*)	8
VOYA	5
Kliatt	3
In-School Polls	2
Other Professional Journals	2

Jay Ruckdaschel, former superintendent of schools who now serves the Association of School Boards of South Dakota, agrees that little attention is given before book shipment: "Librarians have their approved lists like the American Library Association—and from there they make selections."[41]

Atypical is Vancouver Washington's Evergreen school district, which developed a school-board based code of responsible book selection after parents read teen novels aloud to an embarrassed school board.

If the curriculum's controversial, many districts write codes for curricula like sex education, child protection, and psychological testing. Indeed, many states *require* these codes. Among the more recent nationwide codes and bills reported in *The Education Reporter,* Alton, Illinois:[42]

- Lyon County School Board, Nevada: Pupil Rights Protection Policy. All instructional materials "shall be available for inspection by the parents or guardians of the children who will be enrolled. Written consent of the parent must be obtained before students respond to personal questions." (November, 1988).

• Oregon Department of Education: Appointed panel of parents who "strongly oppose, strongly favor, and are undecided" towards proposed nuclear age curriculum, to draft a compromise curriculum. (November, 1988).

• New Jersey Assembly: Upcoming vote on bill requiring teachers to teach abstinence until marriage as the sure way to avoid unwanted pregnancy and infection. (November, 1988).

• Washington State Legislature: "All material directed to children in grades K-12 and providing education regarding any sexually transmitted disease that is written, published, distributed, or used by any public entity and all such information . . . shall give emphasis to the importance of sexual abstinence outside lawful marriage and avoidance of substance abuse . . . " Passed in March, 1988.

• Pennsylvania parents win right to take their kids out of controversial mandatory health/sex education program. June, 1988.

• Alabama: Parents revise sex ed program on state level. June, 1988.

ờ ờ ờ

American parents are beginning to demand a say in what their kids can choose in school. Our own parent reader group responds to this groundswell with a teenage-fiction reviewing tool for parents. But you won't have to spend two years building your case. Using chapter 6: "What You Can Do," and chapter 7: "From California to Ohio . . ." you'll be in the action seat in three months.

From author to reviewers, Anoka media specialist Kathleen Baxter recommends this clean-up campaign for new fiction:

• Christian publishers and editors: Examine the best secular books and seek out authors who write well and with style. If you publish schlock, you give librarians a good reason not to purchase your materials. Give us quality.

- Authors: Show us a view now and then of a child's spiritual life. Maybe that will be easier if librarians would demonstrate that such a view would not inhibit sales.

- Reviewers: Judge these books with an open mind. I often see reviews which state that a biography, for instance, is the only one available on the subject, and is, therefore, recommended until something better comes along. Maybe we have to compromise and do that with Christian books. Most libraries have a paucity of Christian materials. Acknowledge that. Do not be so quick to damn books with the phrase "for church libraries."[43]

3

What We Found, Cover to Cover

Y ou've just finished a novel. Do you know what's in it? You remember the story—but what about the characters? How old are
they? Are they black, white, oriental? Are they blue collar, homemakers? Is marriage dangerous? What does the author think about Life? Are
police the good guys or the bad guys? Are there police *women?* Did you
change your view of the world? Does it matter?

Yes, it matters! Fisher and Small of Virginia Tech quote studies
which say teens may "alter their schema" after reading fiction: When
this happens, fiction has a "profound, often disturbing impact on them."
Studies say teenagers "establish a dialogue between themselves and the
writer."[1]

Are they talking about *one book?* Yes. And if *one book* can have a
profound, disturbing impact, what about your Susie, who gobbles hundreds of books in her room? What about those junior high kids hooked
on "The Master of Horror"?

One high-school father noted his son's growing mound of war, mystery, and horror books over by the dirty laundry and the gerbil cage.
Why did Gordy have such novels? He was encouraged to free-read randomly through a semester of English. He'd squirreled the books under
his bed—gladly paying all lost-book fines rather than return anything to
the library.

So Father began reading too: He read at the same pace he'd seen his
son devour these books—two a day. Three weeks into a steady diet of
psychic phenomena, murder, and war, Gordy's dad became so depressed
he had to quit. This doesn't mean the school library had nothing but

psychic phenomena, murder, and war. But the son had access. No one at school warned him to balance. No one at school pointed him to other types of books. In fact, the librarian said, "All that matters is to get them reading." He even encouraged Gordy with suggestions of similar books! When Gordy's father suggested he use some of their Christian books for reports, Gordy became defensive and embarrassed, "Aw, no one's going to let me read that stuff!"

What This Study Could and Could *Not* Do

We could have analyzed Gordy's stack of books for this project. It was tempting! And isn't that what everyone else does? Just find your list of "bad" books and storm into the school library? But we knew that wouldn't work. We also knew it wasn't ethical: Random selection was our only option. We selected forty-five books from 150 of the top-recommended fiction, and omitted our favorite "objectionable books" as well as our favorite "good" ones. Project-45 was launched.

Our goal? To graph what today's authors tell today's teenagers about the "real world" through fiction, and to work *with* the library to add books for diversity.

We simply tallied what we observed.

Unlike many "reports of findings" from conservative Right or liberal Left, we didn't use "lots of" or "a few" or "probably never." We checked our 110 pages of tallies and 20 pages of raw statistics five times.

But we couldn't study everything. In fact, some things have *never* been rooted out.

No one's studied what American teenagers have just *finished* reading. Ravitch and Finn were the first to graph what older teens remember about literature and history.[2]

This study *does not* tell us what every library in the country stocks for its junior and senior-high fiction.

It *does not* tell us how every librarian uses the promotionals they subscribe to.

It *does not* tell us what teenagers learn from the books.

This study *does* show what's in forty-five new books randomly selected from five of the top lists of recommended fiction for junior and senior highs.

It *does* show what twelve parents learned when they read these forty-five books.

And, separate studies show what's in four different public libraries in four states.

It *does* show how you can use this tool. In three months you can determine if your library fiction gives true diversity.

Tracking the Value Exchange

Values explode like Roman candles in your child's classroom, especially with the move to integrate AIDS education into every subject. Wouldn't you like to chart that exchange?

Reading experts sometimes scoff at parental concern and think we don't want our kids to learn *anything*. But we're not against fair give-and-take. We just question a one-sided sermon that omits the values we've worked so hard to teach our kids. How would *you* answer the experts who say, "Don't bypass controversial books"?

How do we answer Nancy Larrick who says "Books which deal vividly and realistically with current issues can become a positive educational force for individuals and for the community"?[3]

"Reading experts sometimes scoff at parental concern and think we don't want our kids to learn anything. But we're not against fair give-and-take. We just question a one-sided sermon that omits the values we've worked so hard to teach our kids."

We couldn't agree more. But is it realistic in this decade of AIDS and rampant VD to promote fiction (like some of our forty-five books) which says non-married sex is okay? And libraries we checked are running 50–50 in promoting pre-marital sex in those books which discuss sex.

Experts in teenage literature, Nilsen and Donelson say: "Young readers use books as the Afghans use their wedding mirrors. The author acts as the mirror, absorbing directly from life what is of importance and then reflecting this information back to the viewer so that it can openly be examined as *true life never could be*" [emphasis mine].[4]

Experts sweat hard to show us what teens should deal with. Listen to Nilsen and Donelson:

> Psychoactive drugs are readily available; abortions are legal under many circumstances; a college education is no longer considered the panacea it once was; the traditional structure of marriage and family is being challenged as never before.[5]

And to Larrick:

> Fiction and non-fiction about sex, divorce, desertion, drugs, street gangs, poverty, pollution and war may seem bitter fare for the youngster you still think of as your baby. However, these are subjects children get on television, the people and scenes they meet as they walk down the street. Suitable or not, this is life today in the United States. Don't be afraid to discuss the books that can help to make life more significant for your children.[6]

Doesn't that sound convincing? Everyone's telling us what our kids have to "deal" with. But here's where I part company with the experts. If you're going to give our kids real *problems,* please give them real *answers!*

Inside the Books

Come with us. We'll look inside forty-five top-rated teen-fiction books. And we'll see what kind of "answers" are given for those "real" problems. Here's what we'll show you:

1. Do we recommend these books?
2. What kind of writers are these "new fiction" authors?
3. What's on the cover?
4. What's the main idea?
5. Are we talking about long books? Recent books?

6. Are they sexist? Racist?
7. Inside the books, how do they deal with:
   a. Handicaps
   b. Age range
   c. Roles of women and men; family relationships
   d. Race and nationality
   e. Language and style (profanity, literary genius)
   f. Problem-solving tools, (violence, verbal abuse, suicide, God, spirit world, peers, parents, substance use)
   g. Authority figures (clergy, police, government, counselors, teachers)
   h. Relationships
   i. World-life views

**"Do your kids read alone? Our parents
thought only a fourth of these books should
be read without parental input."**

---

1. Do We Recommend This Book?

Our twelve parent-readers had six choices for each book: read alone, read with parent, read with questions, read in conjunction with other books, purchase, don't recommend. But even with six choices, half of these parents checked "read with parents" or "read with questions."

Do your kids read alone? Our parents thought only a fourth of these books should be read without parental input.

And nearly a third said "Do not recommend." Our parent readers' homes bulge with books, but they didn't think any of the novels worth the money! Sure—some are okay for a library outing—but not to cherish—because books at home get read literally dozens of times. (Remember the children's books you memorized with your kids? High schoolers love their books with the same passion. But now that passion might encounter "Jack in bed with Pam" instead of "green eggs and ham.")

How did our parents feel when they'd finished a book? Half were positive, half negative. Some both. Some of us wondered why these authors come so highly recommended!

2. What Kind of Writers Are "Talking" to Your Children?

Aside from best-sellers Tom Clancy (*The Hunt for Red October* and *Red Storm Rising*), Stephen King (*Pet Sematary* and *It*), and Madeleine L'Engle (*Many Waters* and *A Wrinkle in Time*), few authors meant anything to our readers. But to librarians, authors like Max Collins, the Mazers, Susan Beth Pfeffer, Richard Peck, and Margaret Mahy have been old friends for years. Most of the authors we encountered have written at least two young-adult novels.

There was a little Shakespeare in these writers. Readers reported exceptional skill and characters with zest and humor. It wasn't uncommon for parents to appear red-eyed at breakfast after a marathon with Mazer or Clancy. With 80 percent of the books profanity wasn't a big issue. We found good writing, and we were hooked for the duration!

But the language was seductive. It made us side with the hero. A riveting book triggers emotional give-and-take—attitudes change; beliefs alter. A teenager's concept of God can change overnight. From cover to cover, *your child is alone with a skilled author whose beliefs may not be yours!*

Though leaving your child alone with a novel isn't exactly the same as parking your kid in front of a TV, the visual images are the same. The "cognitive social learning theory" developed by sociologist Albert Bandura and others can be used for either TV or fiction. The theory says: when heroes toss stones, smoke cigarettes, or lie, children are more likely to imitate than when a character is "low-status."[7]

3. Look Out for the Cover!

Publishers have one chance to snag a teenager. Blazing book jackets quote big-name personalities and organizations. The language is seductive:

"Distinguished books for young people."

"Winner of Newbery Award."

"An enchanted castle and a terrible secret."

"The horror master's best novel since 1980."

"A romp through some of the roughest, toughest dens of iniquity in the South and Southwest."

"We are talking about the most important work of American fantasy since Stephen Donaldson's *Thomas Covenant Trilogy*."

"Sensitively deals with incest . . . an important book."

You say you've got a child who goes for the pictures first? Here's a picture for you:

A double, peekaboo cover shows a mysterious forest where a young boy glows in the reflection of his magic crystal.

Tough gang fighter Eliot Ness looks knowingly at crime-ridden Cleveland.

A wholesome teenage girl looks yearningly at her handsome warlock boyfriend.

Do Avon publishers think girls need boyfriends more than grandfathers? *After the Rain* plunked Rachel complete with hot pink sweater next to her boyfriend, when this book went from hardcover to Avon paperback.[8] Presto. Grandpa's in the background—not where the author intended.

" . . . a sales representative has only seconds to convince a store buyer that a particular cover will catch the browser's attention."[9]

Stephen King's publishers were so anxious to hook teens that they labeled their characters "teenagers"—not eleven-year-olds: "They were seven teenagers when they first stumbled upon the horror." And *English Journal* said there were *six* kids—not seven. Accuracy isn't the issue.

4. What's the Big Idea? (Themes)

Look at these forty-five book themes. Is this the experts' "life today in the United States"? Here's what we found:

a. Death (25 percent of all themes.) Fifty-one deaths significant to a major character; three holocaust books; death of parents; death of siblings; death of enemies; wholesale death.

b. Peers and Family Relationships (25 percent). A welcome relief, we thought—until we saw death sneaked in as a major or minor ingredient to family relationships!

c. Coming of Age or Personal Quest Theme (25 percent). "Coming of age" means the major character has a masters degree in suffering and ages ten years in six months. She or he matures sexually, emotionally, or mentally and "comes of age" at story's end. These are tied closely to "personal quest" themes; the hero searches for identity, loved ones, or peer acceptance.

d. Good versus Evil (7.5 percent). This theme is as ancient as literature. But two books entwined Christianity with the supernatural so thoroughly that few teens, if indeed parents, could tell the Vine from the trees. The loser? Christianity.

e. Antagonism and Characters Against Society (17.5 percent.) Racism, crime, child abuse.

What We Didn't See: Surprisingly enough, we didn't see books on abortion, teen parenting or AIDS. In our world of teen fiction, apparently extra-marital sex doesn't create such problems! Not one book which portrayed sexual activity said such sex is wrong for teenagers! And for married people? It was a mistake only once.

And if 23 percent of Americans are Christian Evangelicals—or even *half* that (it's been thirteen years since our source was published),[10] why didn't we find any themes about a teen's walk with Christ?

5. Are We Talking About Long Books? Recent Books?

Most teen fiction is less than two hundred pages. You can read it in four bus rides or two study halls. But some of our forty-five books weren't written for teens. One book was over one thousand pages; the shortest was eighty-seven. One was a unique comic book; two were diaries.

Which books are future "classics"? We don't know yet. But the classics among those forty-five books will have a shelf-life of twenty to one hundred years. *After they shape your kids' values they'll pass to your grandchildren. Permanent Connections, Abby My Love, The Changeover, Red Storm Rising, Princess Ashley*, and *After The Rain* are climbing the charts fast, demanding their place in the sun.

6. Are They Sexist? Racist?

Female authors outstrip male authors two to one. Female protagonists are ahead by 9 percent. But totals of *all* major characters (335 of them) show males outnumbering females in the exact proportion reversal: 9 percent! Males outnumber females in both teenage and adult categories.

"With few exceptions, protagonists are Caucasian Americans in modern rural or suburban settings. After a few brief stabs at urban problems in the sixties and seventies, publishers and authors again turned to the country life."

You'll see this formula on TV: Just get a heroine for every hero and you can throw in all the male *minor* characters you want. No wonder some women want to restructure curricula by way of the National Education Association and U. S. Department of Education's "Women's Educational Equity Act Program"!

With few exceptions, protagonists are Caucasian Americans in modern rural or suburban settings. After a few brief stabs at urban problems in the sixties and seventies, publishers and authors again turned to the country life.

(A word about the protagonist: He or she is the *lead* character, the hero or heroine. Besides the protagonist, each book has up to ten *major*—not lead—characters.)

7. Content Counts!

My colleagues say it's heresy to rip apart serious fiction by counting age groups, deaths, or tobacco abuse: "Fiction stands on its own!" But in the name of literary criticism, don't we teach character development, allegory, and "fatal flaws"? The fatal flaw idea means the character's programmed for disaster—it's a standard evaluation tool. It's one I don't buy—we're *all* "fatally flawed."

I have to wonder whether other values shoulder past these book themes—especially if they're class-assigned. What if *Permanent Connections* takes center stage of your daughter's ninth-grade English class? Your Jeanie comes home confused, but you don't know that she's just wrestled with this discussion question:

"Should Rob and Ellie stop having sex when they reconcile?"

Sophomores fresh from a health class suicide film might step into fourth period English and debate:

"Do you think Maus's mother had no choice but to kill herself in *Maus: A Survivor's Tale*?"

(And if you think your teen is strongly rooted in Biblical values, think again. As a substitute teacher I've seen "Christian" kids buckle under peer pressure and the current academic wisdom to "be tolerant of every lifestyle.")

The Universities of Wisconsin and Texas offer television analysis workshops. They count feminine roles in "Dick Van Dyke", angles of champagne bottles on the soaps, and racial slurs in "Gunsmoke." "It's the literature of our age," say professors. "It's the Greek drama of our time"—a kind of "parahistory" of America.[11]

In "the kid with a stone" theory, researchers Patricia Madden and Georgette L. Overby of Prevention Research Bureau in Berkeley, California say kids who see attractive heroes smoking are likely to smoke themselves.[12] We're just counting something your child's going to see, and maybe imitate.

Usually researchers who count things in official laboratories are the ones who get to remove themes they don't like such as smoking on prime time, for instance. That's not our agenda: we'd like to *add* things.

If they can count, we can count.

We count because our teens think we approve of these books. We send our kids to school without challenging curriculum, so, of course, our kids think we agree with fiction's "real life" menu!

Library books are the same as an approved reading list. We want to know what values our kids glean from these "approved lists." If indeed "readers are leaders," the more our kids read, the more they'll absorb these countable ideas. From handicaps to world-life views, every idea promoted in every book will be picked up by some teenage reader. Maybe yours.

Inside the books, here's what we saw.

a. Handicaps: Please, Make It Incidental! We didn't tag emotional handicaps. Most of our characters had them! Instead we let the reader decide. If being fat was the butt of jokes, we called it a handicap. But mostly we counted *irreversible* limitations.

"If indeed 'readers are leaders,' the more our kids read, the more they'll absorb these countable ideas. From handicaps to world-life views, every idea promoted in every book will be picked up by some teenage reader. Maybe yours."

Almost 8 percent of the characters had handicaps—in all sizes and types. But only thirteen handicaps (3.8 percent—and 8 percent of teens) were drastic enough to alter lifestyle.

Over 7 percent of America's school children have handicaps according to the Statistical Abstract of the United States. So teen handicaps are present for roll call in these books. What teen readers *can't* experience in these books is the full range of handicaps for *other* ages.

However, only one book, *Invincible Summer*, has a handicap *theme.* One teen dies. And the other one? She grieves and wonders when it's her turn. Their bittersweet commitment is realistic but comes with a price: teen sex is okay and Robin's view of death is empty:

> Either she would be someplace or she wouldn't. If she wasn't any-
> place, if it truly was lights out, the end, eternal sleep, then what was
> there to worry about? If she *was* someplace, then Rick was there, too
> . . . And so there was still nothing to worry about.[13]

What about the mentally retarded? Of the three characters in our books, only one (*Isaac Champion*) was totally appealing to readers.

Hidden Door gives us two positives: a professor proud of his lemon-oiled wooden leg and our only "legally" blind character.

But here's a switch: portrayed as positive, *Valentine*'s wheelchair character kills his wife by training a dog to attack a necklaced dummy. In the same book, two elementary students murder a frightening retarded boy.

In the 1,000-page *It*, Stephen King's seven pre-teen "losers" love and tease through stuttering, obesity, and asthma. Regardless of what else we thought about this book, King has what it takes to integrate handicap and personality. Actor Alan Toy also pleads for that "incidental" treatment of handicaps. Says Toy: "But we are not by nature evil, pathetic, nor should we be tragic or looking for sympathy."[14]

About a third of the books showed handicaps: and it was just what you'd find in real life. Some good guys, some bad guys—some in between.

b. Age Range: If You're over Fifty, Forget It. If teens read nothing but these books, they'll think the good life is scrunched between ages ten and fifty. There's a self-centered, "I can do it myself" theme skipping through these novels. This "me" approach surfaced in one of my subbing days: nine fifteen-year-old girls talked of "their" rights and "their" future—no one thought of the rights of the babies "their" rights would create. In real life and fiction, it seems, sex begets pregnancy—but not live babies. Sure, we learn about lovemaking in twelve of these books, but we don't get the straight scoop about what comes afterwards. So it wasn't surprising to see these self-sufficient fiction characters getting along very nicely without a bunch of toddlers cluttering their lives.

What happened to the one unmarried fiction teen who *did* get pregnant? She miscarried! (*Bobby Rex's Greatest Hit*).

Here's how these books stack up with the U. S. Census (1987 figures):

Age	Our books	Census
Under 5 years	3.33 percent	7.5 percent
5-11 years	7.33 percent	9.92 percent (est.)
12-19 years	30.66 percent	11.68 percent (est.)
20-34 years	19.11 percent	26.1 percent
35-54 years	30.22 percent	23.7 percent
Over 55	9.33 percent	21.3 percent

Notice that our questionnaire labels nineteen to thirty-five-year-olds "young adults." Recent educational doublespeak dubbing twelve- to eighteen-year-olds "young adults" is one more step in what attorney John W. Whitehead calls "adultifying" our nation's youth. Teenagers may be "young people," but they are not "young *adults"!*

In all forty-five books there were only fifteen infants and pre-schoolers. The good news? Readers thought them mostly positive.

Two-thirds of "older" people took a beating. All-around "best" in this category is *Many Waters'* Lamech (the biblical Noah's father). He'd had 782 years to perfect his image!

Most golden-agers were crabby or demanding. There were a couple of exceptions, like *Goodbye's* "older kin"—sort of gruff and gentle though a bit too much given to spicy language.

Ellen Foster's grandmother was the worst of the lot: "She was hateful, vengeful and cruel—there was nothing about her I liked!" said one reader. This sick woman was every youngster's nightmare. After suffering through her vulgar tirades and nursing the sick woman to death's door, Ellen describes the final scene:

> I just stood by the bed and looked at her dead with her face pleasant now to trick Jesus.[15]

c. Roles of Women and Men and Family Relationships.
Is it the old double standard—or the new?

When I read three hundred of my own kids' books ten years ago, I thought stories were unfair to women. They were. That prompted educators to say, "Let's leave out homemakers": Come picture-taking time in America's new textbooks no one told the stay-at-home mother to come for photographs. Updated textbook pictures say women who once rocked babies now remove gallbladders and fly planes. Paul Vitz saw this as just plain bias in his textbook research:

> Traditional roles for both men and women receive virtually no support, but feminist portrayals regularly show women engaged in activities indistinguishable from those of men. Finally, clear attacks on traditional sex roles, especially traditional concepts of manhood, are common.[16]

This reverse sexism began in the late sixties (didn't everything begin then?). Sociologists began their microscopic study of women's roles.

What they found resulted in a searing backlash that's now reverse sexism in full flower.

Today's hip sociologists use government statistics that say mothers who work "full time at least four weeks *per year*" are officially "full time." If these temporary workers are counted correctly, however, we find *only 20 percent of pre-school American mothers leaving home to work.*[17]

But the children's stories studied by Vitz, and Project-45 books, tell a different story. Although the forty-five books say 36 percent of all adult *women* and 50 percent of *mothers* are homemakers, *a third of them are from other countries and time periods! Only 14.5 percent of these fiction mothers are positive contemporary American homemakers—the ones teens could use for role models.*

Like Vitz, we found gross inaccuracies. Could these novels teach our children moral *truth* if they fail in statistical averages? (Don't believe the censorship rhetoric that says books can't hurt your kids: An entire branch of science, bibliotherapy, says literature profoundly affects kids. This new science is regularly used to change attitudes. For instance, if your child just lost a loved one, the librarian or favorite teacher might be tempted to steer her towards several "death" books in the library. My 1986 research of one school's elementary library books showed that not one fiction book on death gave heaven as the final destination!)

Our random forty-five books say the first thing fictional mothers did right was go to work. Teen-fiction Moms don't do just any old kind of job, either. Most are white collar or self-employed. *This is blatant misrepresentation:* glamour jobs may be the stuff of teen fiction, but not for real working women.

Ironically, over half of our "good" mothers were dead before story's end (*Maus, Ellen Foster, The Return, What Niall Saw, When The Phone Rang, The Goats, Eyes of the Dragon, Invincible Summer, Loydene in Love*).

Wives who left hearth and husband to "fulfill" themselves (*Bobby Rex's Greatest Hit, Dark City, Goodbye, Permanent Connections, Rich in Love, It*) weren't as much to blame as their male counterparts. In fiction, women always had good reason to leave; men didn't.

Paul Vitz in *Evidence of Bias* documents children's readers that switch traditional male and female roles. But is it any wonder this switch occurs? In directive after directive state departments of education continually tell your kids' teachers: "Remove gender stereotyping from the curriculum." If "stereotyping" means "traditional roles," the directive to "remove it" means "change real life"! A closer look at Alvin Toffler's traumatic *Future Shock* (1970) is a shock in itself: This book doesn't *reflect* real change or even *supposed* change—*it's a blueprint*

---

*"Only 14.5 percent of these fiction mothers
are positive contemporary American
homemakers—the ones teens could
use for role models."*

---

for change! (How many of our self-centered couples of the seventies followed Toffler's advice to exchange a "child-cluttered" marriage that could be "streamlined" by two working people?[18]

But let's be fair. Look at the "outdated" children's books. Moms stayed home but didn't have fun. So it's no surprise that the new teen fiction shows Moms leaving home for good times.

Authors and publishers, I have a challenge for you: show creative, adventurous homemakers! If you're looking for role models I can show you a few hundred. *Rich in Love*'s mother got her kicks from ditching the family to "find" herself. *After the Rain*'s Mom is dumpy and tearful. With such role models, no wonder young women cop out of homemaking and jump into business suits. When we tell young girls, "You can be anything you want to be," we subtly suggest they choose *anything* but homemakers.

Double standard? Check any lately-published sociology index and you'll find "sexism." Sometimes it says, "See feminism." That's because today's sexism is what's done to women and not what's done to men.

But Bernard Goldberg says this double standard is alive and kicking. "Men are the newly insulted" he gripes. He objects to the new double standard which tells us to quit stereotyping females but leaves no place to put men except in traditional female roles.[19]

We found a lot of Bernard Goldberg's reverse sexism in these forty-five books. What he objected to on TV we saw in teen fiction. When we could *find* fictional fathers (if they hadn't disappeared, died, or deserted), they were 14 percent nastier than mothers. Husbands were slightly better than fathers, but they weren't as "nice" as wives (who had it rough, considering their brutish husbands). Only single men got balanced treatment.

Near the top of the brute list was the incestuous dentist in *Abby My Love* (it deals fairly and sensitively with incest, but the "Dad is bad" theme is still there). In *The Changeover,* one father deserted his family for a younger woman and the second abused his foster child in the name of the Bible. And just when you're beginning to like the father in *Tricksters*, you uncover his adulterous past!

Some young characters spent whole books just looking for wayward fathers (*Denny's Tapes*; *Sons from Afar*; *What I Did for Roman*); or parts of books (*River in Winter*). Other kids couldn't search for Dad because he was dead or long gone (*The Crossing, The Return, Good-bye and Keep Cold, Corky and the Brothers Cool, Strictly for Laughs, Abby my Love*). Some kids doubted their dads cared for them at all (*If I Were You, M. E. and Morton, The Year Without Michael, Princess Ashley, Hidden Door, The Goats, Eyes of The Dragon, Greencastle, Circus Day*).

Some dads just slapped their kids or wives or else hurled insults (*Isaac Campion, Jimmy D., Ellen Foster, Greencastle, River in Winter, It*).

"Nice" fathers just hung around smiling appropriately or being careful not to spoil fun.

But now look who were the "good" Dads: A Russian officer (*Red Storm*); the pastor who let his son make his own mistakes but whose wife thought him selfish (*Corky*); the older brother who sacrifices school and postpones his sleep-in girlfriend to nurture orphaned siblings (*When the Phone Rang*); Chelsea's warm but emotionally crippled father (*Princess Ashley*); four strong patriarchs from generations past (*Seventh Son; Many Waters, It*); the tough father who sent his son to help sick relatives, but who would rather spring his son from jail than let him take a drug rap (*Permanent Connections*); and the usual assortment of strong war heroes (*What Niall Saw; Eyes of The Dragon; Maus*).

d. Races and Nationalities. Populist or Melting Pot? Only 5.4 percent of *protagonists* (lead characters) are black. The percentage of *all* *black characters* in these books is better—10.7 percent, but still this comes short of the 12 percent national average. While these fictional blacks are missing a couple of percentage points, they're *80 percent positive!* In fact, only two *minor* characters were negative—and that puts the amount of time devoted to positive fictional blacks even higher.

Maybe this overly-positive treatment of blacks is the token salve for the scarcity of blacks in general. Problem novels and race riots exploded into our world at the same time—the sixties. Publishers squirmed and took a hard look at their equal-opportunity fiction. They scrambled to close the gap, and for awhile it looked as if fiction might be more census-accurate.

But powerful black novels like *A Hero Ain't Nothin' but a Sandwich* left some parents and educators reeling. Spouting profanity and leaving good and evil choices up to the reader, this highly controversial novel didn't do much to promote black fiction.

Black author John Steptoe mourns, "Interest disappeared rather quickly. It almost seemed like a particular day. It was as if the publishers got together and said, "Okay, enough of that."[20]

Steptoe thinks earlier publisher interest was "just a flash in the pan."[21] But the 1985 and the 1989 updated *Literature for Today's Young Adults'* "Honors Sampling" is more than a flash in the pan. The 1985 "sampling" of the best books between 1967–1983 shows *17 percent black protagonists*. The 1989 text shows almost identical percentages.[22] By contrast, we found only *5.4 percent black protagonists* in our forty-five books for 1988.

The hard questions: Did earlier professionals deliberately balance ethnic groups in their "honors" lists, or did these previous honors sampling books with black protagonists truly compete favorably with other choices? Conversely, were some excellent books omitted from today's lists because, as Steptoe says, "the industry is inherently hostile"?

The Black Church in Teen Fiction

And where's the Black church—what Taylor Branch calls the "Old Testament prophets"? Branch says these prophets are key to black culture "identification."[23] With twenty million black Christians,[24] or *8 percent of our total population,* where is the "outcry" of Christian blacks in our teenage fiction?

Calling himself a "black, liberal Democrat," former sixties civil rights activist Dr. Lorenzo H. Grant, pastor of the Breath of Life Seventh Day Adventist Church in Fort Washington, Maryland, *does* cry out—against "glamorization of illicit sex, crime and violence (on TV) . . ." Amazed to find himself in the same camp as conservative American Family Association's Donald Wildmon, he says, "By the time the jury is in we will have lost another generation, and perhaps something even more precious—our national soul."[25]

Our two African novels *appear* to be on the right moral track. There's no mistaking the black South Africans' legitimate apartheid lament in *Waiting for the Rain*. And black Jews give us a clear, positive message in *The Return*.

But wait a minute—where are the black *Christians? The Return* (set in Ethiopia) describes black Christians as vicious, Jew-hating bigots. Ted Veers with Sudan Interior Mission, former missionary to Ethiopia, says these "Christians" aren't from the churches he knew: "The Ethiopian-born Christians I know would never treat their black Jewish neighbors with such contempt."[26]

Hispanics

They were just as negative as blacks were positive. There weren't very many of them to begin with—just 3 percent of all characters (and only one of them a protagonist). *But they were a shocking 73 percent negative.* The one Hispanic protagonist (*The Crossing*) is mostly "positive," but this book (and *Corky*) was sprinkled with other bad-guy Hispanics and left readers "depressed."

In our forty-five books *we saw no American Hispanic protagonists.*

And What of Orientals?

If it hadn't been for the *Asian-American* pilot in *Red Storm Rising*, we'd have seen zip of this ethnic group. Does teen fiction mirror national jealousy of Oriental-Americans? "Today, American-born Chinese work in much the same occupations as white Americans—but with a greater degree of success."[27]

And with our resentment of Japanese economic coups, it isn't likely that Japanese-theme fiction will sell. We saw one Asian-American: Clancy gave us an Asian woman pilot in *Red Storm Rising*.

"With twenty million black Christians,
or 8 percent of our total population,
where is the "outcry" of Christian blacks
in our teenage fiction?"

Stories from the sixties and seventies included Asian refugee themes—publishers knew we'd root for them. But now? Asian-Americans are carefully saving their street-corner vending profits and winning top scores on S.A.T.'s: Are we still cheering? Educators may hope to champion "realistic" and "controversial" teen fiction as one key to adolescent social growth, but publishers test the economic wind.

Native Americans Didn't Fare Well

One positive cameo role in *Seventh Son* was all we saw of this group. King's near-fatal Indian smoke ritual (*It*) didn't do much to boost Native American charm either.

A Mohawk Indian pastor in New York and Canada says native Americans are forgotten citizens. Minorities lists usually omit this group, giving "invisible status" to "America's indigenous people"[28] The teen books we saw were proof of his claim.

But younger kids' books? Take a walk through any public library's *elementary* section and you'll see more native American than African-American themes. Now check out the plots: these native American stories come loaded with spiritual overtones, usually at the expense of traditional Christianity. Teacher Ken Roberts' ordeal over Bible-removal from his school mirrored the bias: The principal said it was okay to teach about Indian religion, because they pray to a rainbow goddess and not to Jesus (See chapter 2).

e. Language and Style: Is It Ever Okay to Swear? Even though three-fourths of our books had some profanity, only those 18 percent of books with frequent obscenities impacted our readers negatively. However, *totally positive* reader response to *occasional* profanity was just 60 percent.

Halfback Tough (from a professional reviewing service using high school readership polls) has locker room characters but no locker room language! It was strongly believable—and popular with kids.

By contrast, that same readership poll gives us Stephen King's *It*, which lets seven elementary kids wallow in enough vulgarities to top an R-rated chart (you didn't hear these censored profanities on network TV's November, 1990 remake of *IT*). Are we supposed to believe these fictional kids would spew expletives in small-town 1957? Our reader said no to suitability.

Aside from two "simplistic" books, we were dazzled by author skill. For instance, writing like this doesn't need profanity:

> The September day was so blue—that intense blue that makes you ache inside, and I got thinking about modifiers. They live hidden away, I decided, gray slimy things like leeches, spending all their time multiplying until harvest time, when English teachers dug them up and stuffed them between the pages of grammar text books.[29]

Curiously, authors had their own brand of profanity, and stuck to it. Some had vulgarities like "f___" and "a___le." Some profaned deity (God, Jesus, Mother of God, G_dd___t).

I asked my readers: Should we quote profanities? We agreed: If our twelve-year-olds face vulgarities in school fiction, we should face it too. *Some public school children read more profanities in one semester of "personal" or "individualized reading" than their parents would read in a lifetime.*

Indeed, it was thirteen-year-old boys who jerked me awake during one of my subbing days: "Why can't we swear in the halls, when library books have lots of dirty words?"

"Tell you what." I said. "Ask the administration."

Maybe we didn't like the profanity. Maybe we didn't like the no-fault sex. But in these forty-five books we knew polished verbal skill when we saw it! Spiegelman scored a hit with his surprise comic book genre (*Maus: A Survivor's Tale*). The lilting Polish/Jewish accent for cartoon pigs, cats, and mice literally mourns in this Holocaust theme: "At that time it wasn't anymore families. It was everybody to take care for himself" (p. 114).

Rich in Love sparkles with artistic surprises:

But I could see how it might happen to someone whose interior life got out of hand. Like a little fox in the dark, with sharp teeth and claws, the secret life will gnaw and gnaw.[30]

f. Problem-Solving Tools: Don't Leave Home Without Them. Problem-solving tools work best in problem novels, which exploded on the teen scene in the mid 1960s. These novels give quick problems and quicker choices in a fast-paced, predictable formula. Popular Judy Blume books are good examples.

If new fiction gives real problems, what are the tools they use for solutions? The new literature teaches "life skills" along with good writing, and too often good writing takes second place! What are these skills? How do the "new" fictional characters solve their problems? With alcohol? Peer support? God?

Just Say NO? Substance Use

Dare we suggest that one or two books a year might change how a teen thinks about beer and cigarettes? We believe these books *can* change a teen's way of thinking, because kids are trained to see the school as an authority figure. Anything on school shelves is official *knowledge*. It's "Education" with a capital "E."

Since the mid-sixties a growing number of school texts avoid special-interest group wrath: They do it by omitting actual historical references to America's Judeo-Christian heritage. Fewer and fewer teens attend church or synagogue. Schools vote out commencement prayers. What fills this vacuum? An ever-shifting sand dune of relative values— and books are a large part of the message: No wonder those eighth grade boys got mixed signals!

Characters use twenty-two problem-solving tools in these forty-five books: 11.2 percent of all tools are a combined casual use of alcohol, tobacco, and drugs. We got the message: this use was *okay 50 percent of the time.*

But there were no substance *abuse* themes, which we would have welcomed. Abuse themes would have come down hard on casual use and its subliminal message.

Teens—Take Center Stage!

By far the biggest problem solver was support from people. Of those "others," peers and siblings rated tops. The next choice? "other adults." Not parents.

Did teens and kids ever lean on parents? Sometimes. Here's the twist, though: *Leaning on parents had twice the negatives and only half the positives of the other choices.*

Most fiction puts teens center stage. They're wise, wonderful, witty—and long-suffering under the hands of misguided parents. *This subtle shift away from adult-centered classics gives your fifteen-year-old nothing to grow up to!* Most fictional parents are left with co-dependency "concern and caring."

Three-fourths of characters leaned on "significant others"—not parents. After your child reads *Rich in Love*, will she follow this advice: ". . . sooner or later a child will realize love is more wisely invested than in a parent."[31]

If It's Okay with Me, It's Okay:
Situation Ethics and Manipulation

Situation ethics is at the very core of those "values" philosophies created by the demise of moral absolutes in the sixties. Quite simply, situation ethics means that lying is okay if it's okay for *you* at the right time. Manipulation, which most authors used as a *negative* character trait, is what happens when other people's values don't agree with yours. It's the end result of the Dewey creed which says there are no God-given absolutes. John Dewey, the modern "father" of education, wrote a large chunk of *Humanist Manifesto I* in 1933.[32] Much of our "critical thinking" education comes from his doctrine that each child creates his own good answers if given enough time, patience, and education.

Situation ethics got higher marks than manipulation. This tool took fourth place among all twenty-two tools (taking 8 percent of the total). It's this philosophy that gave *Permanent Connections* a surprise ending—at least it surprised our readers: Lawyer and father know it was Rob's marijuana in the truck; but they're ecstatic when the judge frees Rob. The situation dictates: *Truth isn't as important as staying out of jail.* Rob and his friends see no moral absolutes denying them sexual pleasure, either.

Over the past two years I've seen *Permanent Connections* in lots of junior-high classrooms and libraries. In this skillfully written, family-centered book, both teachers and students might swallow these "relative" values with barely a twitch of the Adam's apple.

Books like this are more subtle than simplistic grocery-store romances. Why? It's the educational setting which puts its stamp of approval on such books. It's the two-week language arts "unit" which dubs it valuable. And it's the "achingly beautiful" writing that gives it credence.

"We believe these books can change a teen's way of thinking, because kids are trained to see the school as an authority figure. Anything on school shelves is official knowledge."

We found other slippery values. *Corky's* lead character lies, cheats, and steals. Sure, we're "supposed" to figure it's wrong. But Corky's lying was so often and so convincing that his victims became fools. And what reader wants to identify with a fool? Our parent reader (a teacher herself) said: "I felt sorry for manipulated teachers!" And *Corky's* minister loses his effectiveness when his wife deems him self-centered.

Jimmy D., Sidewinder, and Me is a situation-ethics marathon. How could a ten-year-old reader discern right from wrong in Dumas' naively wicked story? (*Publishers Weekly* recommends it for ages ten and up).[33] Dumas pleads with the judge:

> It wasn't so much that I wanted to be a pool hustler, your honor, but you remember how I'd been sent to live with the Rhoduses as a kind of punishment, and I told you how I'd been saving my money to run away; well, this was my chance.[34]

And what about gambling?

> There's something about gamblers . . . children want to grow up and be like us; and a woman will fall in love with us at the drop of a hat.

. . . What we are is what she wants—adventure, romance. And if we tell her to, she'll leave her honest, hard-working husband in a second and follow us anywhere. ["This statement sums up the message of the book," said our reader.][35]

And *The Goats*? It was strict upbringing which made the stripped, peer-kidnapped thirteen-year-olds leave I.O.U's every time they stole something in their desperate escape odyssey. And our thumbs up to this author, who knows the elusive trick of getting readers to identify with both sets of generations!

God—One Big Blur

One reader said, "figuring out God as a problem-solving tool was like bottling a fog bank." This tool got the lowest "positive" ratings— even lower than "violence" and "verbal abuse"!

Most readers simply threw in the towel and noted "blend" when tallying this tool. This sums up the forty-five books. God is a foggy blur. Rob's encounter with a priest in *Permanent Connections* comes closest to making God real—but it was mixed with the fuzzy concept of "talking to the God in yourself, the holy place within."

Besides *The Return*'s Jewish heroine, and to some extent *What Niall Saw*'s child hero, there's no *protagonist* relationship with a personal God. (Noah in *Many Waters* wasn't a protagonist. The two teenage boys were.) In the forty-five books, with minor exceptions, God is at best a weak crutch—not a living tool. "Who is He?" the authors seem to say. After forty-five books we wouldn't be surprised to hear an author complain, "If I give God more than a hint of credit, I won't be published!"

But for "reasoning," there's no such confusion. Only two negatives marred this second highest of all tools. The gray area ("blends") received only 15 percent here.

Like James in *Sons from Afar*, most characters say "I'll work out my own problems!":

> He'd be OK, if he didn't get lost from himself along the way. Francis Verricker, he thought, had gotten lost. [Referring to his father who left the family.] How, or why, James didn't know, and he never would know, he guessed. But that didn't matter for James. It was up to James to see that he [James] didn't get lost.[36]

Conjuring Up "Helpful" Spirits

Praying to "My Lord Mithras, Master of Light" happily occupies two younger kids' playtime (Joan Aiken's *If I Were You*). And four high-school boys in *Greencastle*, calling themselves "The denizens of the Sacred Crypt," conjure Egyptian gods in their secret meetings. Harmless fun? *Greencastle* was flip about it, and *If I Were You* treated the Mithras exercise as if it happens to nice kids every day.

The Changeover was just that—changing over from mortal, every-day high school girl to witch. After all, it was the only way she could save her little brother from a life-draining hex.

**"This sums up the forty-five books.
God is a foggy blur."**

The kids in *IT* chose a confused mish-mash of occult rituals to bash their mortal enemy—an extra-terrestrial spider. What's strange about *IT* is to see heroes fighting spirits with occult tools. What teen is spiritually astute enough to untangle this web?

Seventh Son is a beautifully-written glimpse of the "other" nine-teenth-century America. There's something like magic. No, it's like witchcraft. Wait a minute, I think it's Christianity. Let's see, the minis-ter vows to kill the boy because he's possessed. Or is he? What's the matter with "good" magic? Wait a minute.

But waiting a minute doesn't help. There's only one story which comes close to untangling the confusion we get from these forty-five books. *Many Waters'* two protagonists warp into Noah's time so we can see deep values of family, honor to parents, and virginity. It does startle one a bit, though, to see the supposedly "changed" teenage twins put drivers' licenses and home-cooking as their first priority upon returning home.

Does Fiction Suicide Promote Suicide?

If only 60 percent of the "suicide" tools were negative—that means that somewhere in these forty-five books, suicide *isn't* negative. In fact of the ten suicides there was one positive suicide, three "blends," and one decision *not* to end it all (*When the Phone Rang*). We didn't count Shilda's miscarriage, even though the book made it seem as if the pre-born wanted his own death (*Bobby Rex's Greatest Hit*).

You can't get to legal first base trying to prove that novels, Dungeons-and-Dragons games, or heavy-metal music prompts your teen to suicide. But Tipper Gore says the link may be there:

> Suicides and suicide attempts increased dramatically in a two-week period immediately following the showing on television of four fictional movies about suicide. . . . the study did not determine if the victims had actually seen the movies, except in the case of one 17-year-old New York boy who watched and then copied the manner of suicide.[37]

And Pat Pulling in *The Devil's Web* says her own investigation of son Bink's satanic suicide leads increasingly to a connection between satanic symbols, literature, heavy metal music, and ritualistic, dangerous cult activity. Authorities who used to scoff at satanic crime links now see all parts of the teen satan scene as so dangerous that gang activity seems like a nursery rhyme in comparison.[38] The teenage suicide trigger is hair fine.

A pet seal's death triggers suicide for the unstable sealkeeper in *What I Did for Roman*. Roman challenges God to rescue him from inside the lion's cage, where he holds a suicide vigil. Darcie, duped into joining him, tells Roman the newly arrived guards are rescuing "angels." But she can't talk him out of his Daniel delusion, and he is brutalized at dawn by a set of very hungry felines.

Billy fares better (*When the Phone Rang*). He talks his sister back from the roof. Young readers will thrill to the way he lures sister Lori from a precarious apartment ledge:

> I squatted down next to her, my arm awkwardly across her shoulders.
> "Give me your hand, Lori." Her fingers knotted against me. . . .
> "Remember when we were on the roof and I said I loved you?"[39]

Stan (*IT*) wasn't lured from suicide's brink by a friendly hand, however. In the sanctuary of his closed bathroom, his wife never hears him slash his arm in a gory rebuke to the monster who ravaged his sense of order. Writing "*IT*" on the tiles, Stan dies rather than face the world's disturbed pattern.

It isn't so much the suicides as the value-system in which they're cast. If a teen reads about suicide, don't you want him to know a God-centered reason *not* to follow through?

Vengeance, Violence, and Verbal Abuse

This tool didn't get much use—little over half as much as "support from people." But just as we'd expect in our good guys/bad guys culture, vengeance got more positives than negatives. *Combined* vengeance, violence, and verbal abuse was 15 percent of all tools. It was gratifying to note so much aversion to personal violence. Most authors avoided it as their main theme.

> **"It was gratifying to note so much aversion to personal violence. Most authors avoided it as their main theme."**

But *Ellen Foster*, *IT*, and *I Remember Valentine* are riddled with verbal abuse. *Valentine* also gets high violence marks. The notorious Hart family—sporting such first names as Big, Broken, Lacey, Valentine, and Black, give us a mild sample with their every-day family dialogue:

> Lacey turned to the boy they called Black and lowered her face to his, putting her beautiful soft nose close to his bloody one. "If I ever catch you tormenting that cat again I'll beat the h__ly s__t right out of you myself."[40]

We saw two kinds of violence: wholesale and personal. We tallied personal violence only. That's how a world-scale shoot-em-up like *Red Storm Rising* gives low tallies for violence as a problem-solving tool.

What Niall Saw is another such book. Though it personalizes wholesale violence, no major character is violent. Seven-year-old Niall's diary takes us under the family stairs as they hide from "the Bomb." In painful non-comprehension, he pens a baby sister's slow death and a God and parents who can't help.

Red Storm Rising is the technical reader's dream. There are enough bombs to satisfy the most avid mercenary. Millions die. But we get more technical detail (probably more than we ever wanted) than blood and gristle. The horror of violence is lost in the thrill of weapon description.

If you want enough gore to last you through the next century, *IT* is the book for you, and violence is the tool of choice. Arms, legs, and noses fly everywhere—unearthly creatures dart for parts of your body you forget about except when you bathe. Voices and blood burble up the sink drain—clowns maim—old photographs slice fingers. One of our readers tells of her teenager's horror at reading Stephen King's other works in 1984: "I just filed it away—I couldn't deal with it. It freaked me out!" King truly is the "master of horror." But maybe you don't want your ninth grader getting a masters.

Yes, it's a violent world. And we don't want to shelter our kids from this fact. But a recent study showed that *males were more likely to act out what they read, saw, or heard when violence and sex were linked.* Males who are exposed continually to such scenes believe that women *want* violence—that sexual arousal comes from sado-masochism, such as we saw in one book.

Violence as a *positive* tool took only 2 percent of all tools. However, it was used negatively less than 60 percent of those times.

We shudder to think how high the violence rating would have soared had we tallied every missile button push in every war scene. But we tallied personal violence only.

g. Roles and Authority Figures. Doctor. Lawyer. Merchant. Chief. Tinker. Tailor. Beggarman. Thief.

Children have chanted this jump-rope rhyme for a hundred years: Listen carefully to the rhyme—we're playing it out in our class-conscious society.

Want to make it in this world? Get a white-collar or self-employed job. America's *perceived* power is the mirror image of that simple jump-rope chant. That same perception—though statistically inaccurate—was reflected in our books—57 percent of adults employed outside the home wore white shirts in our books. Only 11.5 percent were blue collar, and although 62 percent of the "blue collars" were positive, that's an abysmal showing. Even worse: Only 7 percent of all jobholders in these books give blue collar workers a positive image.

The self-employed got top billing—67 percent positives. Lots of our fictional mothers were self-employed—as were 21 percent of all employed for pay.

"Only 7 percent of all jobholders
in these books give blue collar workers
a positive image."

Women aren't penned as secretaries anymore either—only 5 percent of our fictional work force showed up in pink collars. Less than half of them were positive.

Farmers took the blue ribbon. Maybe this reflects the 1980s sympathy for farmers: these books are the "Farm-Aid" of fiction. Two books were "commercials" for organic farming! (We wondered: what if Christianity had been given the same hard sell as organic farming? Would those books have made the "best-rated" list?)

Readers didn't have trouble telling the good guys from the bad guys in this category—not many "blends" here!

Without Benefit of Clergy

Of all the bad guys, "clergy" took worst-of-show. There were "hamster-like" ministers, "evil" pastors, "lewd" clergy. And one who waited a half hour before tumbling into bed with his newly-evangelized striptease artist. Our two best pastors were brief cameos: a briefly-described minister who drives James and Sammy to the train (*Sons from Afar*), and the New York pastor who gives Jody 1 Corinthians 13 to begin her healing after the family's kidnap trauma (*The Year Without Michael*).

Corky's Dad was diminished when Mother spoils his image.

After *Waiting for the Rain*'s scathing indictment of white South African churches in general, we jumped at the chance to try to like that book's one specific South African minister. But he was powerless (or didn't know where to get power). As a white, he wasn't able to help blacks.

This odd assortment of clerical bumblers snags only 3.7 percent of the positives in the authority-figure lineup!

Town Fathers—(No Town Mothers)

"Peacekeeping" and "government" topped the good-guy chart. *The Goats'* vulgar sheriff, who handcuffs two teenagers to the pickup, the bad cop in *Dark City*, and *River in Winter's* loathsome sheriff are the three exceptions. Aside from these, we're more likely to see kindly police like the one in *M. E. and Morton* or good guy Eliot Ness in *Dark City*.

School's Out

Teen characters spent a lot of time at school and made underhanded cracks about the instructors. Those teachers took 35 percent of the authority figures list.

We're sure some of our authors are under-cover English teachers: Note their subtle (and commendable) attempts to lure readers into good literature. A character "casually" mentions a good book or quotes Shakespeare. Harry (*Greencastle*) is obsessed with reading, and author Lloyd Kropp handily describes dangerous "concerned mothers" whose main evil is stamping out dirty books. In a heroic soap box oratory, *Greencastle's* Jewish bookstore owner shames ministers and "concerned mothers" for this censorship madness.

Organizational leaders—camp counselors, sports leaders—were sparse. At the top of this bunch was *Halfback's* wise coach. No profanity. No Pollyanna sweetness. Just cast-iron tough commitment.

h. Relationship Expressions: Have You Hugged Your Kid Today?
Most parents in our books would say no. Parents and kids touched only 10 percent, and *I Only Made Up the Roses* was a big chunk of that. *Roses* is a seventeen-year-old's memory of her biracial family. This story swells the heart with touch. But the book has no plot—we think few teens would read it.

Greencastle shocks us with a teenager who's willing to touch his mother: Calling her "my beautiful Mommybuckets," he distracts her while she's driving until she declares she should have been a nun.

Squeezing arms and occasional "falling into a mother's arms" were about it for touch. Our fiction fell far short of the recommended three hugs a day. Even physical violence was low; whether hugging or slapping, touching just didn't happen.

Kid-on-kid violence was low too: Kids squared off only 7 percent of the time; 85 percent of those times was negative. Siblings socked each other about as often as parents/kids (4 percent).

How do parents and children feel about each other? Nearly half showed positive commitment, concern, and obedience, but it was mostly a lopsided set of strokes, with parents doing most of the good stuff. Parent-child interaction cornered a fourth of all relationships.

Safe Sex?

With so many fictional parents running around, we expected more marriage models. Not so: marriage took only 10 percent of all relationships. Everyone's worried about TV's distorted marriage roles. But take a new look at your teenagers' school-based fiction:

- Faithfulness in marriage is okay only 75 percent of the time.

- Unfaithfulness is okay 20 percent of the time.

- Violence and verbal abuse are in 10 percent of marriages.

- Commitment is okay only 40 percent of the time.

- Sexual intercourse occurs outside of marriage almost five times as often as within marriage.

New fiction's petting and sexual intercourse aren't in the marriage bed. They're on mountain tops, tunnels, and car seats.

One of the longest sexual descriptions is in Stephen King's *IT*. In a ritual attempt to foil the alien monster's power, six elementary school children take turns having sex with willing eleven-year-old Beverly. She doesn't get pregnant. She recovers immediately. Undeterred by marriage commitment, it isn't surprising that twenty-eight years later she encores with two of them.

Only one girl is pregnant from non-marriage sex (*Bobby Rex's Greatest Hit*). Conveniently, she miscarries.

No one gets herpes.

Or gonorrhea.

Or syphilis.

Or chlamydia.

Or AIDS.

Only one (a married man) regrets the act (*Circus Day*).

"In modern times, few people speak of 'committing adultery,'" says Annette Lawson in *Adultery*. In her study, less than a third of participants even *use* the term "adultery." And the Lawson's standard? A bit on the gray side.[41]

Our books weren't gray. No one thought adultery was wrong. *Circus Day*'s father "regrets" but doesn't moralize.

Flannery O'Connor's essay, "Total Effect and the Eighth Grade" bemoans dragging fourteen and fifteen-year-olds into modern literature before they've studied more traditional works. Writing in 1963, she says current fictional adultery "is an inconvenience" at best.[42]

How many of our fictional characters "live together" sexually? Just 24 of 335. They have a not-surprising 10 percent commitment rate and zip for concern and caring! Sexual intercourse is their main diet of expression. Except for one graphically violent sexual romp, these couples aren't memorable.

What Works?

Employment didn't produce good role models either. Boss-employee relationships had the most violence. Just a fourth of employees commit to fellow worker or boss, and without emotion. No concern and caring here.

But there's good news: If you want work ethic, check out James and Sammy (*Sons from Afar*) and Prince Peter (*Eyes of the Dragon*). James and Sammy's fishing business would make any teen eager to try a little after-school work. This work ethic wasn't widespread, however; only 12 percent of fiction teens juggled jobs and school.

i. What in the World Are World-Life Views? We hit quicksand on question 10, because our goal in the beginning was to list every religion in the world! Impressive. But we were sure to leave out someone's favorite.

With amazing simplicity, Pastor Al Kuiper of the Christian Reformed Church (Hull, Iowa) rescued me with the concept of world-life views. Here are four views of the world, and I challenge you to find any known religion that doesn't fit very nicely into one of these:

1. *Impersonal spirit or gods-centered life view.* Gods or spirits are indifferent or hostile and need to be placated or manipulated.

2. *Personal God-centered life view.* One, all-powerful God created the world and is lovingly involved with his creatures.

3. *Object-centered life view.* Fate or undefined "forces" control life.

4. *Person-centered life view.* People have increasing ability to solve problems without outside interference or help.

These views were even smoother in practice than on paper. Readers could weight them in four frequencies and choose more than one life view for each book.

"Sexual intercourse occurs outside of marriage almost five times as often as within marriage. New fiction's petting and sexual intercourse aren't in the marriage bed. They're on mountain tops, tunnels, and car seats."

After reading forty-five books, it wasn't hard to list the "religious rules" of young adult fiction.

It was okay to: Refer to God in allegory. Describe faith in some other culture. Ridicule pastor or priest. Let the character ask faith questions. Give power to minor gods.

It *wasn't* okay to: Give real faith answers. Make God a major part of an American teen's life. Give pastors or priests Godly power. Ridicule the occult. Ridicule a rabbi.

A fourth of all Americans claim to be Evangelical Christians. A fourth of these books' world-life views reflect a "personal God." So what's the problem?

Let's look deeper.

Nationally, one-fourth of Americans see God as a vital and *positive* part of their lives.

Our teen fiction says Christianity is a negative!

So you want better polls? There's more: Consider the polls from *Operation World* and *100% American*. *Operation World* says 87 percent of Americans believe in God (p. 434). *100% American* says some polls show that 83 percent of Americans feel close to God, and only one percent of Americans do not believe in God.[43]

Our teen fiction says just the opposite! In these forty-five novels a personal God took only 10 percent of all positives and more than half the negatives! Fate or impersonal spirits had 20 percent of the positives. Person-centered had 61 percent of all the positives. Person-centered had only 7.3 percent of all the negatives!

These books feed us the exact opposite of what the American people express as their beliefs, and therefore their needs.

These are peacetime polls. How much more do we need a "faith" book in World War III holocaust stories like *Red Storm Rising* and *What Niall Saw*! The spectre of killing half the world's population surely brings slayer and victim alike to their knees. Fifty years ago, *Parents' Magazine* said, "Religious books always come when there is a war."[44]

Though *Red Storm Rising* isn't about nuclear war, as the review mistakenly announces, this techno-thriller's "conventional" arsenal would obliterate us just as neatly. With all this blasting to bits, we wondered why no one prayed. Forty-five years after World War II, we still hear fresh tales of prayer-wrought miracles for battle-stressed soldiers in France, Africa, China, and England.

Our Jewish character Desta asks for God's help in *The Return*, and she gets it. We wish *The Return*'s Christian bigots had asked for the same help.

Niall (*What Niall Saw*) asks continually for God's help in his childish, misspelled diary. God's answer isn't what he'd hoped for, in this post-nuclear calamity.

Ravitch and Finn say our teens don't know basic Bible stories. They say children must know Bible facts in order to understand everything from *Time* magazine to political cartoons. How many teens saw the humor in a February 1988s cartoon of George Bush (Goliath) lying stunned from a flimsy reed? Bent straw in hand, Pat Robertson was a smiling "David."

It's a good thing *What I Did for Roman* specifically tells us Daniel is the guy who wound up with lions, because 40 percent of America's seventeen-year-olds think it was Jonah who was tossed in the den.[45]

Likewise, L'Engle was smart to cast Noah in *Many Waters,* because he's one of the few Bible characters recognized by nine out of ten students in the Ravitch-Finn study. But aside from Noah, the Twenty-Third

---

> *"New fiction's literary 'heart' died when fate took over. It died when any meaningful God-centered experience was forbidden entrance to teenage literature."*

Psalm, David, the Creation Story, and Moses, seventeen-year-olds failed in their answers to almost every other Bible question.

Campus pastors lament the continual decline of Bible knowledge. Incoming freshmen lack commitment to God and church. University extra-curricular groups—and the administration itself—compete with campus ministries for the formerly sacred Sunday and Wednesday "church days."[46]

Do "churched" high school students do any better? They've invested three years of "confirmation" or "Decision" training. What do they know after a lifetime of Sunday school? In 1988, thirty such students didn't know the difference between humanism and Christianity. "Why can't you be a humanist *and* a Christian?" was their response to a one-hour "Secular Humanism and Education" seminar. Ten years of person-centered public education had done its job: Our kids were the proverbial frogs atop the Bunsen burner. Students mistook the heat of death for the energy of enlightenment.

Strictly for Laughs, a comic masterpiece, sums up the jumbled Bible, spiritist, and person-centered lingo most kids glean from thirteen years of school. Our comic heroine Joey pretends to hang herself, then "mutters frantic prayers to Jehovah, Allah, Osiris, and Zeus."[47]

Two black South Africans at the University of Northern Iowa agree their countrymen are deeply religious. Christianity is a regular part of

South Africa's *public* school training. These college students vehemently agree Christianity is their country's answer. South Africa's black Christian pastors would jump at the chance to agree with these dreams for Africa's future in the American media. *Waiting for the Rain* didn't give them space either.

Instead, nihilism and non-answers—death and life—are wrapped in pantheistic packages throughout teen fiction.

"Death of the Heart, American style," reads *River in Winter's* book jacket. This ironic prophecy was born out in the statistical averages of these forty-five books. New fiction's literary "heart" died when fate took over. It died when any meaningful God-centered experience was forbidden entrance to teenage literature.

After reading these 45 books, we saw "Death of the American expression of God." If these books truly reflect the ideal of fiction to "help us understand ourselves and develop our personal values,"[48] we're in bigger trouble than we thought.

4

The Project Forty-Five Books

Y ou've seen the books as a whole. Here they are one at a time.
Though the reviews may hint a bit, for the most part, we withheld judgment.

Please. Read the books yourself. Make up your own mind.

Best Books for Young Adults, 1987
(American Library Association)

The Crossing, by Gary Paulsen
(Watts/Orchard/Richard Jackson, 1987)

Son of an American father and a Mexican prostitute, fourteen-year-old Manny fights for daily bread in Juarez, Mexico.

Passing him unnoticed is brooding Sgt. Locke, in Mexico to drink away the troubling voices from dead Vietnam buddies.

They meet when Manny tries to heist Locke's wallet. Though Locke is moved to feed Manny the biggest feast of his life, his help is perfunctory: The ever-present "voices" have taken over, clouding compassion.

But Locke finally sees Manny's plight and plans an illegal border crossing. A violent street gang of Mexican "wolves" (teens) jumps the unfortunate Locke. Manny, encouraged by the dying Locke to grab the wallet and run, makes it to America.

In a dirty Mexican alley, Locke yields to death as a soothing balm, where he finally meets his "voices."

The Dark City, by Max Allan Collins (Bantam, 1987)

This thirties thriller features Eliot Ness against bad cops and underworld con men. Against the backdrop of Cleveland's gray winter, Ness struggles with a failing marriage and instructions to wipe the city's slate clean.

Having let his wife slip away for lack of commitment, he faces a new conflict of interest: should he give his sleep-in lover the big "L" just because she's the bad guy's daughter?

Ness finally gets his man—the "Inside Chief"—the dreaded bad cop. This fast-paced yarn is ripe with 1930's street talk—not suitable for the seventh through twelfth grade summer reading list.

Denny's Tapes, by Carolyn Meyer (Macmillan/Margaret K. McElderry, 1987)

Denny's white mother remarries—and stepsister Stephanie, the darling of her white daddy's life, oversteps her limits by snuggling with Denny.

So, tape recorder in hand, seventeen-year-old Denny records a cross-country, soul-searching journey to find the black father who deserted them and a deeper understanding of his biracial heritage. His college-educated, quick-tongued black grandmother in Chicago fills him in on their family's accomplishments and introduces him to sexy Roxanne, who educates Denny without textbooks.

Denny plays it loose, absorbing each experience as it comes. But his toughest stint is at the hands of bigoted Christian Nebraska kinfolk and his white grandmother—whom he rescues from her emotionally abusive, church-going family.

And when he finally gets to San Francisco—it's too late. His father's gone again. But in his father's apartment, the ghosts of his music past come alive: Denny sees a music career for himself as well. He decides to stay in his father's city—holding before him like a beacon the thought of "Philadelphia!"—his and Stephanie's secret code for their future consummation.

Ellen Foster, by Kaye Gibbons (Algonquin/Vintage, 1987)

At eleven Ellen sees through all the shame society pitches her way. She sees her mother die from her abusive father's neglect. And when it's her turn to be abused, she runs.

And she writes. With colorful language she learned from her father, his poker buddies, and her wicked grandmother, Ellie peppers her diary with deadly accuracies. From the safety of her new foster home, she flashes back to one painful trauma after another.

Though forced to slave with her grandmother's black laborers, Ellen's real abuse comes from Grandma's profane and vulgar tirades. With steely toughness Ellen discovers she's the only nurse to her grandmother's fatal illness. So she commits herself to service and adds her own touches of humor.

Until her final safe home with her "foster" family, black school-friend Starletta remains the only constant in a life of abuse and uncertainty. Though written about an eleven-year-old, this book belongs in the adult section.

The Goats, by Brock Cole (Farrar/Straus/Giroux, 1987)

Two young teenagers, dubbed "goats" by fellow campers, are stripped and abandoned on the camp's deserted island. Realizing their only hope is with each other, Laura and Howie escape and swim to the mainland.

Howie's parents are too far away to join the search, but Laura's mother lands in camp prepared to find her own clues. Author Cole's skilled pen drops us with equal comfort in both Laura's and her mother's shoes.

More afraid of real life than the unknown, Laura and Howie break into a summer home, steal a teenager's beach clothes and smuggle aboard an inner city camping bus—seeking both inner direction and distance. The two youngsters cling to family values in tight spots, and their prolific I.O.U.'s help muffle stealing and trespassing.

When Laura's mother finally catches up, the solution doesn't come easily. A tough new Laura holds Howie's safety as her ticket to return, and the hand stretched out to Mother is reluctant and conditional. An exceptional glimpse into the minds of social outcasts.

I Remember Valentine, by Liz Hamlin
(Dutton, Pocket Books, 1987)

This loud and sassy novel pits eleven-year-old Valentine and her new friend against their opposite cultures when the Depression puts them in the same apartment house. The book's young narrator steels herself to shed inhibitions and accept some of the gems beneath her neighbor's raw surfaces.

With impossible names like "Broken" (the handicapped result of a failed coathanger abortion), "Lacey," "Big", "Valentine," "Sweet," and "Black," the infamous Harts educate their little neighbor about sex and poverty. The parents—Big and Lacey—never wait for privacy before groping beneath each other's clothing, and Valentine lets her parents have it with both barrels of vulgarity when crossed. Amidst the poverty and filth, Valentine's little neighbor feels more acceptance from the Harts than from her own proper and aloof mother.

There's more training to come, as Valentine and her friend conspire to murder a retarded neighbor, and Valentine's handicapped employer trains his dog to kill his wife. So it isn't surprising that one of the little narrator's last acts is to show her body to Black in return for silence. It turns into a felt as well as seen experience, complete with the mysterious callings of womanhood. Later her friend urges Valentine to forget her near-rape from the retarded Gurney and "give in to it (sex). . . . making love is a lot like telling lies—the more you do it, the better you get at it" (p. 309). This book is not a "Best Book" for young adults—or for adults, either.

Isaac Campion, by Jannie Howker (Greenwillow, 1986)

The backdrop of this turn-of-the-century English story is as gray as the smokestacks behind Isaac's horse farm. Always there is premonition—of brother Dan's death, of father Sam's lurking vengeance, and of Isaac's desire to run away to America.

Told through the eyes of ninety-six-year-old Isaac, this tale lets us see viewpoints of teenager and old man alike. Young Isaac works hard but must constantly dodge his irascible father's temper.

With new babies and overwork, Isaac's mother spreads her comfort thin. Isaac is caught between the desire to grow up his own way and the need to please his parents.

The traditional country religion isn't much help, and Isaac finally admits to his mother that he doesn't believe the Lord is "just." Brother Dan's accidental death at the hands of a local teen consumes father Sam

Campion with vengeance and pushes an already jeopardized family over the brink.

But Isaac waits to catch that steamer to America until he sees his father's new horses safely down the river—his sense of duty deep. Ninety-six-year-old Isaac now looks back, sorry that his father died, sorry that he didn't have a childhood—and wishing that in the next life he could come back as "a swift or a swallow."

Jimmy D., Sidewinder, and Me, by Otto R. Salassi (Greenwillow, 1987)

At fifteen, Dumas Monk has seen almost all there is to see. From orphanage to exploitative foster family to gambling dens—he sees cheating, drinking, religious bigots, fast women, and murder. And now the judge asks him to write it all out. Thus the book, which begins, "Dear Judge Francis, your honor."

In twenty-five letters Dumas justifies most of his actions. He likes the gambling, drinking, and the women who taught him a few private lessons, but he isn't party to cheating and murder. Refreshingly free of profanity, this book explores the pits of 1948 society.

The gambling life, though dangerous, is glorified. It's not hard to guess that "Judge Francis, your honor" will let him go, and Dumas will snag in a new web of adventure before he's dry behind the ears. *Publishers Weekly* recommends this book for "ages 10 and up." (July 24, 1987, p. 134).

Many Waters, by Madeleine L'Engle (Farrar/Laurel Leaf, 1986)

Sandy and Dennys fiddle with their mother's lab computer and trigger a sonic boom. They wake up in Noah's time, peopled with small, mammoth-like creatures, diminutive humans—and evil, embodied spirits (the "Nephilims").

Though the story sometimes falters under the sheer weight of its complexity, L'Engle makes Noah's time come alive—just in time for the Flood. Twins Sandy and Dennys realize with horror that they may be swallowed up, and Noah's youngest daughter with them.

In this book of revered elders, solidly rooted marriages, and respect for virginity, there is also a clashing of good with evil and the tiny triumphs—by the twins and Noah's family alike—that add up to a satisfying Victory.

Deftly choreographed is L'Engle's second time warp, which raptures daughter Yalith to heaven, and Sandy and Dennys home on the backs of unicorns. Though they admit they are "changed," the twins respond to the familiar comforts of baking bread and fresh cocoa with a purely teenage thought: when to get their drivers' licenses.

Princess Ashley, by Richard Peck (Delacorte/Doubleday, 1987)

Chelsea doesn't want anyone in her new, upper-class high school to know that her mom's a school counselor. And she's a little ashamed that her emotionally weak dad raises dogs. So it isn't long before she falls prey to the charisma of "Princess" Ashley—the girl who has it all.

Peck's amazing knowledge of high school cliques makes this standard "problem novel" believable. As Chelsea's Ashley-worship reaches its peak, she finds herself in over her head—Ashley wants "just the right party" to foil the senior class, and Chelsea's property will do very nicely. Chelsea sees her error sooner than she makes amends, however, and it takes the final tragedy of a friend's drunk-driving accident to bring her around.

Chelsea's off-beat boyfriend with the flower generation parents can take a bow for helping her dig beneath the surface. So can Chelsea's mother, who gives her just enough rope to bring her to her senses. Real human problems with real human answers.

Seventh Son, by Orson Scott Card (Tor/St. Martin's/Tom Doherty, 1987)

Someone—or Something—doesn't want the seventh son of the seventh son to be born. Faith Miller, her labor already begun, barely survives the raging floodwater to give birth to this "miracle" child. But whether this is truly a "seventh" son is open to question: Faith's son Vigor is swallowed up in the raging torrents in the very struggle to save the new baby.

And there are more questions: If little Peggy's a "Torch" who saves seventh son Alvin's life, are her powers "good" or "bad"? Does the stiff-necked, prim preacher do a good deed or a bad one when he tries to kill Alvin? Is "hexing" a harmless, primitive piece of Americana, or is it a work of the devil? A traveling storyteller, "Taleswapper," tries to add sense to these gray areas by saying that things aren't always what they seem.

In this traditional pioneer land where Father is patriarch and kinfolk stick together, we see another dimension in this superbly written tale—it's a society where traditional Christianity and "magic" rise side by side. And magic, in the guise of good son Alvin, is the winner.

Sons from Afar, by Cynthia Voigt (Macmillan/Atheneum, 1987)

Despite having a mentally ill mother and a deserting father, James and Sammy have it pretty good. Grandmother wisely models independence and hard work, and older sister Dicey adds her parenting skills. But James, the thinker, wants to know his past. He wants to know why Gandhi said, "Western Civilization would be a good idea." He wants to know why "normal" kids can't see that it's the "dorky" kids who grow up smart.

He wants to find his father.

Finagling a day trip to Baltimore, the two boys follow leads from the library, an old teacher of their father's, and instinct. Their journey ends at a seedy bar, where they discover they're not the only ones who want Mr. Verricker.

James and Sammy don't find their father, but they find each other, and learn to make allowances for their vast differences. This book is about more than love, it's about commitment.

Through the Hidden Door, by Rosemary Wells (Dutton/Dial/Young Readers, 1987)

At his exclusive boys' school, twelve-year-old Barney parts company with five delinquent friends. Thus begins a war with the schoolmaster, and dangerous hours of solitude. But social outcast Snowy shows him a diminutive kingdom in an abandoned cave, and the two loners strengthen their inner world with the thrill of discovery. Their questions prove far more exciting than schoolwork:

What kind of snake produced the wickedly powerful venom they found on the ritual fang? Was it left by the historically-documented religious fanatics who tried to prove worth through immunity? If the tiny, perfect city in the cave wasn't made by tiny people, how did the marble steps get worn in the middle? When you've trapped five taunting schoolboys in a cave, should you abandon them, knowing their death would stay secret?

Barney gets no answers from the cruel, Bible-reading schoolmaster; his refuge is from former headmaster Dr. Finney and wife Dorothy. But he'll never know who really lived in that tiny city, because a bizarre turn of events transfers him to another school. Junior high kids will identify with the loneliness of the outsider, and with looking inside yourself to solve tough problems.

Waiting for the Rain, by Sheila Gordon (Watts/Orchard/Richard Jackson, 1987)

Nine-year-olds Frikkie and Tengo love the South African sun, the security of family, and carefree life on the farm. But while Frikkie skips his way towards white manhood with uncaring steps, Tengo broods more and more over the cruel injustices of apartheid.

Tengo's rage over his family's obeisance to the white man takes him to the city, where he sees side-by-side "justice" played out at every level. The author skillfully shows the white man's brand of caring and Christianity, and the enslavement it brings. Tengo begins to think his answer is with a revolutionary cousin.

A final street fight leads these two old friends to an abandoned warehouse, where they become new enemies. Frikkie the soldier sits wounded while Tengo decides his fate. Though Tengo spares Frikkie, very little mending takes place, as the real anguish has years more to play.

What I Did for Roman, by Pam Conrad (Harper and Row, 1987)

With a flowing hint of mystery, Conrad shows us Darcie's heart—for her lost father, for her new love.

While employed at her aunt's zoo cafeteria, sixteen-year-old Darcie searches for the father she never knew—the one who thought she was a "beautiful baby." And the troublingly mysterious, handsome Roman helps her find another side of herself when the sealkeeper's favorite animal dies. In despair, Roman chooses a creative exit to life: He would challenge God to save him from the "den of lions," and take Darcie with him.

But Darcie's life is knitting together in light of her new discovery: Though the father she never knew was dead, he had loved her. She will not throw that away in some romanticized lion-cage suicide. She tries to show Roman his biblical error, but he chooses death. She chooses to live for her father's good name.

Aside from a moody, alcoholic uncle, this story provides many positive adult role models. The short biblical discussion among circling lions is instructive—and hair-raising.

What Niall Saw, by Brian Cullen (St. Martin's, 1985)

It's 1990-something, and Ireland's just been hit with "The Bomb." Seven-year-old Niall starts his diary, while we look over his shoulder.

Woven with family images of caring and humor, the aching loss and sense of doom magnifies with every page. Niall's quaint misspellings and lapses are harder and harder to read as radiation takes its toll. And who would not be frightened as Niall faintly calls, "God plese helps us—[sic]," and nothing happens.

Though fear of the Bomb seems to be Cullen's main concern, readers will be bolstered by Niall's commitment to his little sister and to his parents' sacrifice for them all.

Books for Children and Young Adults
(*School Library Journal*)

M. E. and Morton, by Sylvia Cassedy (Crowell, 1987)

"She wasn't dumb and she wasn't crazy. She was magic, just as she had always said."

The summer of her twelfth year, M. E. meets a strange friend. She says exactly what she wants and wears leftover clothes. She makes M. E. do things she'd never dreamed of doing before. M. E. thinks she has this strange friend Polly all to herself. But Polly prefers M. E.'s retarded brother Morton, and presto—M. E.'s lifelong sibling jealousy is out of the bag.

This cleverly crafted book talks straight to young readers about learning disabilities, about growing in your own strength without peer pressure, about speaking up to a mom and dad who don't understand you, about creating a fantasy world with none of the old, tired rules.

But there's a big gap in this story: Why wasn't Polly accountable for the off-beat way she tempted Morton to retrieve a toy from a building ledge, never telling anyone she knew where Morton was hours after they'd searched for him?

The reader is left dangling with the terrible thought that Polly's "magic" revival of the comatose Morton exempts her from accountability.

The Return, by Sonia Levitin (Atheneum, 1987)

In 1985 thousands of black Ethiopian Jews were airlifted to Israel from Sudan. This is the story of four of them. Ethiopian "Christians" blame these "Falasha" Jews for their country's woes. Any moment, these Christian nationals could bring calamity to teenage Desta's village.

So Desta, her little sister, her big brother, and her fiance walk through Ethiopia to the unknown—through death, hunger, and fear. In the Sudan, thousands are flown out. But thousands die in camp—and Desta, with God as her constant companion, continues her care of little sister Almaz.

Levitin writes from a heart schooled in Nazi prison camps. Perhaps she knew God there—and now she helps the young reader see Him again through Desta's return to the promised land: "I emerged at last, empty of tears, full of Someone who had enfolded me and answered, 'Desta, I see you.'

"I had returned."

After the Rain, by Norma Fox Mazer (Morrow/Avon, 1987)

Rachel's grandfather is dying. Rachel discovers a new boyfriend. Rachel wonders if she can survive her fifteenth year with all this and smothering parents too.

Rachel's a chronicler. Chubby, out-of-date parents, wayward older brother, grumpy grandfather—all are glaringly memorialized with Rachel's ruthless pen. But Rachel begins to see her own worth through reaching the heart of an old man—that old man who finally unlocks her world of feeling and "called her darling."

Through that new sense of worth her chronicled characters receive a muffled forgiveness.

Though *School Library Journal* says *After the Rain* is "poignantly reassuring," one is not assured of life after death—this Jewish family leaves hope in the hands of people.

The Year Without Michael, by Susan Beth Pfeffer
(Bantam, 1987)

Brothers aren't supposed to disappear between home and the softball field. But fourteen-year-old Michael does. This horror compounds the pain of near divorce in the dysfunctional Chapman family.

This book is about real problems and real people. It's also about answers that don't work: Bumbling police who wait too long to find Michael; shouting matches in a crumbling family; blaming God for Michael's disappearance. As the reader wades through family alienation, shouting, and fear, this story begins to look like a horror story of lost hope.

Sister Jody, sixteen, in one last desperate attempt, hops the bus to New York, hoping to spot Michael on the streets. What she finds is an open church door and a minister who gives her a Bible verse: "Love endures all things . . . and never ends." That thought gives her hope.

We're not sure whether this is the hope her parents cling to when they finally admit, "You know the only way we can have a future together is if we get help."

But we know in the end what kind of "love" never ends for Jody. It's the love she feels for the lost Michael: "[It] burns steady in those moments, and it illuminates my life." If this is a story of intervention by a personal God, it's one with endearing touches, but no real power.

The Tricksters, by Margaret Mahy
(McElderry Books/Macmillan, 1986)

It's Christmas week in New Zealand—and summertime in this inverted world of seasons and spirits—of ghosts and talking imaginations.

Crying out for wholeness, the Hamilton family bypasses the strength of Christmas for a tryst with three strange brothers—coming like "three wise men" to their vacation beach home. Are these young men three parts of the long-drowned Teddy, or are they embodied spirits of seventeen-year-old Ariadne's imaginings?

Whoever they are, they trigger a Christmas Eve catharsis in the family: One of them makes love with Ariadne on the beach, and Ariadne's father later admits his adultery with a family friend. But there's forgiveness, and an uneasy acceptance of what the three brothers brought into their lives. The reader sometimes feels like Ariadne's mother: "I know, I just know there's some trick in all this, and if only I can get the hang of it our lives will end up better for it all, richer and stronger . . . But I'm reduced to crossing my fingers."

Teenagers may not get the hang of it either. But we can hope that Ariadne's next story, written under "the witch's cap" of her summer home, will give the answer.

Best Adult Books for Young Adults
(*School Library Journal*)

Bobby Rex's Greatest Hit, by Marianne Gingher (Atheneum Ballantine, 1986)

It's hard to live in a small town when you're the subject of the latest Hit Parade song. Against a backdrop of the fifties and sixties, Pally Thompson works through her memories of remote, handsome singing star Bobby Rex and what it was he said she did with him behind the creek that night.

Gingher provides breathtaking sensory pictures, like illusory run-on sentences. Woven into these grand illusions are kids, mothers, and ministers lustfully bending the rules and finding the experience beautiful. The happy ending with the young girl marrying the veterinarian isn't enough to dilute it.

If I Were You, by Joan Aiken (Doubleday, 1987)

Can we do it? I run off to Christianize India, and you be my father's daughter while I'm gone? It just might work, if others thinks we look as much alike as our mirrors. So begins a nineteenth-century English switch that opens school-girl Alvey to the challenge of remolding a stubborn family with firm love.

Aiken makes a strange plot believable, and leads us willingly into the living room of her lively characters—from the lascivious clergyman to remote and depressed parents, from wise grandmother to epileptic, courageous Tot. The ending is a reminder of Daphne Du Maurier's cruel turnabout in *Scapegoat.*

In true romance form the ends are neatly stitched despite missionary Louisa's untimely return to claim her family place. Young readers can appreciate the exhilarating story line, but Christians may be disappointed by Louisa's selfishly motivated missionary zeal, and the younger children's obeisance to the god Mithras.

Maus: A Survivor's Tale, by Art Spiegelman (Pantheon, 1986)

At last! A teenager can read a comic book without hiding it inside a textbook. Spiegelman's cartoon genre boldly revives the Holocaust with mice as Jews, cats as Nazis, and pigs as Poles. Son Artie sits with his father and step-mother to record flashbacks—and present-day images.

Though Nazi violence is the underlying theme, all the accompanying deception by friends, uprooting of families, and Artie's own wrenching account of his mother's later suicide vie for center stage.

Young readers may be entertained by the comics, but they'll also have to face unresolved guilt, a failed marriage with no solutions, and whether to accept Spiegelman's view of pre-marital sex.

Red Storm Rising, by Tom Clancy (Putnam/Berkley, 1986)

This technical masterpiece lures us into the middle of World War III with no place to run. Moscow makes the first move: Their oil refineries ravaged by Muslim terrorists, they pull a gory sting to capture Europe's wealth and sabotage America's retaliation. This is not about nuclear holocaust, but conventional warfare at its worst—and macho readers may think—its best.

Though brilliant weapon descriptions and trans-Atlantic legerdemain are Clancy's trademark, he sidesteps these to portray a Russian father's fears, the American husband's lonely duty, and a reluctant civilian's bravery.

This is an adult novel reviewed for young adults. God's name comes up frequently, but not for help.

Iowa Teen Awards 1987–1988 Masterlist

Abby, My Love, by Hadley Irwin (Atheneum/Signet, 1985)

Chip can't understand why Abby, his love since junior high, withdraws into moody silences. One day he discovers her awful secret, and this shocker sets the stage for an unusually sensitive novel about sexual abuse. Hadley Irwin (two women authors) craft a much-needed probe into an increasingly common horror. It's done with a minimum of profanity and only enough suggestion for readers to "get the picture." Readers will appreciate Chip's description of his new love: "Listening to her was like listening to the engine of a finely tuned sports car."

Abby's problem is answered with family therapy, time, Chip's love, and the sensitive support of Chip's mother and her boyfriend. Though Abby's family is "not religious," Abby's final assessment of her father's act is refreshing: "He wasn't sick, Chip! . . . He was wrong! He did something terribly, terribly wrong!"

Buddies, by Barbara Park (Knopf, 1985)

Fourteen-year-old Dinah has one good friend, an okay sister, two loving parents, a devoted dog, and good looks. So why would she risk everything to join the "in" crowd at summer camp? Barbara Park's deftly comical dialogue makes us uncomfortable with the excruciating pain of social misfit Fern, who attaches herself to Dinah at Camp Minnewawa.

Desperate to rid herself of Fern and make herself look good to new friends, Dinah pushes Fern into the lake. She then begins the long road of rationalizing her behavior. We can rationalize right along with Dinah, because Fern's character is so continuously disgusting that young readers will see little worth redeeming. Dinah prays, but for selfish reasons. She finally asks Fern's forgiveness but is rebuffed. Dinah is filled with guilt until she remembers something she learned in a science class: Everybody makes mistakes, and that's okay if you learn from them. "Eventually you've got to forgive yourself for the stuff you do wrong or you'll go crazy," she comments to herself. Among other things, this book may be about forgiveness, but it's not God's.

The Changeover, by Margaret Mahy (Scholastic, 1984)

When you're fourteen and your little brother's been hexed by a demonic shopkeeper, it's tempting to look past the usual answers. Especially since Laura's father skipped out on the family and her mother doesn't quite catch onto things.

So it's not surprising that Laura succumbs to a good-looking warlock and his mother's and grandmother's eerie way of doing things. It's simple, really—you just go through a counterfeit baptismal rite, with candles and blood-red images, and emerge a witch with powers to zap the shopkeeper and reverse the hex. If Laura had any qualms about being a witch, they're stilled by remembering warlock Sorenson's childhood abuse by a Christian foster father.

With little brother safely unhexed the suggestion is that newly bewitched Laura and warlock Sorenson will make love "sometime," but marriage isn't mentioned. Maybe Laura's willing to dismiss the marriage alternative because her mother has a sleep-in boyfriend.

Margaret Mahy's fans won't be disappointed by her broad metaphors and comfortable dialogue. She is also skilled at combining witchcraft with respectability.

Corky and the Brothers Cool, by P. J. Petersen (Delacorte/Dell, 1985)

Tim, the minister's son, leads an uneventful small-town life until "cool" Corky invades his domain. Then it's anything goes, as his fast-talking friend leads him to lie, cheat, and steal. The reader is pulled between despising Corky and believing he's right.

Tim's father listens well and lets Tim make his own decisions. But when Tim and Corky think "anything goes" as they renovate a junked car to woo a girlfriend, Dad calls a lie a lie and a wrong a wrong. He prays with Tim and makes him promise he won't repeat the offense. But Tim's mother is quietly resentful: She thinks her husband gives everything to the congregation and shortchanges the family.

This story is about morality, about "cool" kids and ministers' kids. If you "give people a chance, they'll turn out okay." But Corky didn't turn out okay, and finally left town. Tim admits he didn't change either. This book is a disappointment in its treatment of Hispanics and to the belief that God changes lives.

Strictly for Laughs, **by Ellen Conford
(Pacer/Putnam/Berkley Books, 1985)**

Comedienne Joey hopes for big-time broadcasting, and love interest
Peter is just the one to get her there. Enter Dinah, for a laugh-filled love
triangle that keeps you guessing until the last chapter.

The fast-paced easy dialogue hides shallow character development
and little choice of role models besides self-centered teenagers: There
are no wise adults waiting in the wings. Instead, our protagonist jokingly
invokes all the known gods (Jehovah, Allah, Osiris, and Zeus) to do her
bidding when she feels herself going off center stage. The brief, tender
love scene, though satisfying, seems a little awkward in a story in which
most lines are a breath away from Barnum and Bailey's clown act.

When the Phone Rang, **by Harry Mazer (Scholastic, 1985)**

It was a typical Saturday evening in the Keller house. Until the phone
rang: now three kids have no parents.

This is no syrupy tale of kids making it alone. They wade through
junk food binges, social service surprise visits, sibling fist fights, and a
backfired apartment renovation. Despite Billy's suspenseful and loving
attempt to rescue little sister from her suicide jump, this book shows
teens for what they are—not quite adult enough to do a parent's job.
This is a no-nonsense book about real problems.

But for all the realism, it's still depressing to know that teenage
Billy's solution to dealing with death is, "No one will save you, there's
no one to blame, no one to hide behind."

Since all the answers are inside Billy, some readers may guess that
his real problems come after story's end.

University of Iowa's Books for Young Adults Poll
(*English Journal*)

Circus Day, **by Caroline Crane (Dodd, Mead and Co., 1986)**

Kate and Ted have a perfunctory marriage—kids, suburbs, the whole bit.
While Ted spices his marriage with an out-of-town fling with a female
co-worker, Kate is having another kind of adventure.

Too willing to be nice to everyone, she unwittingly tells the stranger in the mall parking lot that her husband is out of town. Moments later she and her kids head to Vermont, hostages in their own car.

Their stint with violent escaped cons is a nightmare of physical abuse and psychopathic uncertainties. Meanwhile, Ted comes home with a guilty conscience and a missing wife and sets out to find what's left of his family. In the final moments daughter Candy's little circus hat—stuck to a backwoods Vermont tree—leads Ted to a heart-thumping rescue. A fast-paced gripper with more than enough prison language.

Don't Blame the Music, by Caroline B. Cooney (Pacer/Putnam, 1986)

Susan's sister Ashley didn't make it as a rock star, so she's come home to make somebody suffer. Susan's in the way. What begins as Ashley's bizarre acts of vandalism on her sister's jeans, jewelry, and bed ends with near murder.

Susan calls on God, parents, and boyfriend for help and admits her boyfriend does the most good. Then, Susan's father finally decides to have Ashley committed. But Ashley beats him to it, owning the decision herself in a final, sobbing breakdown.

Though the title implies a different sort of blame, it isn't hard to blame the drugs, alcohol, and heavy metal culture in Ashley's past because here is a loving, disciplined family, staying together in spite of it all.

Getting Even, by Susan Beth Pfeffer (Pacer/Berkley, 1986)

Annie Powell's spoiled from her summer internship on the prestigious *Intern* magazine. The only thing that will keep her senior year from being a complete bust is editorship of the school newspaper, a position she thinks is in the bag.

But the school advisor has other ideas, and Annie begins to think her only job now is to get even. Her huffy pride very nearly destroys her after-school job and new college boyfriend.

Annie's grandmother is a wise ally, helping Annie aim for more moderate solutions. While she's at it, Annie also gets her father to understand how her mind operates, and broadens herself with the book, *How to Make Your Anger Work for You.*

Set in the Northeast, this book is loaded with ivy league names and upper-class professions: Annie applies to Princeton, Stanford, and Yale. Her parents are both professors. Her boyfriend's an ivy-leaguer. One should have such problems! Well written but simplistic—appealing to younger teens. Though the profanity was minimal, it wasn't necessary.

Halfback Tough, by Thomas J. Dygard (Morrow, 1986)

Joe makes a fresh start in his new school, and overnight he's a football hero. But his old lifestyle of drinking, smoking, and wild parties comes back to haunt him when two old buddies come to town. The inevitable happens: he's accused of breaking into the school.

Though vaguely characterized, his parents seem understanding—letting him make his own decisions.

In the final clash of Joe's new and old self, Joe calls it quits. It's the last game of the season, and he knows the team would be better off without him. It's the cast-iron coach who guides him to a lifechanging decision in this macho football thriller.

Of all the surprises in this book, here's the biggest: It's a locker-room story without locker-room language.

IT, by Stephen King (Viking/Signet, 1986)

In 1957 Derry, Maine, the beast from the "Deadlights" is killing children. Masquerading as a clown, burbling up in sink drains, inhabiting a giant bird, this monster is known only to seven sixth-grade "losers" who hang out in the town marsh. In a final showdown beneath the city, the children—six boys and a girl—cut hands for blood unity and join in ritual sex to gain cosmic power. Thus the beast lies dormant for twenty-eight years.

When the killing resumes, Stan in despair cuts his wrists in the bathtub, writing "*IT*" in a bloody talisman on the tiles. The remaining six adults reunite to thwart the monster.

Although unusually sensitive to handicaps and social outcasts, this book comes with a price: It is one thousand pages of profanity, creatively hideous violence, graphic sex, and anti-Christian symbolism. We think few adults could handle such a book, but maybe we're wrong: King dedicates this story to his three children—all under fifteen.

Loydene in Love, by Lael Littke
(Harcourt, Brace, Jovanovich, 1986)

Loydene's in love. Maybe. Before she jumps out of high school into a rural Idaho marriage, she wants a working vacation in Hollywood to set her straight. She meets suave Jakey on a movie set and almost succumbs to his charm.

Back home with fresh perspective, she realizes the rock-solid worth of her childhood sweetheart, U-Haul. She wants to join her life with his. But she chooses to wait, having seen the bondage of friend Roxanne's single parenthood and the suffocating urgency of filling a new home with parents' belongings and parents' decisions on the home ranch.

Good problem-solving tools, with no profanity. Mormons will recognize the Latter-Day Saints' value system and view of heaven.

Young Adult Editors' Choice
(National Council of Teachers of English)

The Eyes of the Dragon, by Stephen King
(Viking/Penguin/Signet, 1987)

In this fairy tale, ugly is evil and beauty is not; black is bad and white is good. King adds another dimension: youth is wisdom. Set in a mythical kingdom of Anglo-Saxon Middle Ages, this tale pits an ageless sorcerer, Flagg, against the young heir apparent.

Peter's gentle mother raised Peter "to be good." Above all else she hated the attitude of "who cares." She is Flagg's first victim. When Peter is framed for Flagg's next murder (the King), he's confined to a high tower, and the bumbling twelve-year-old brother is Flagg's stairstep to power.

Peter's childhood dollhouse is the key to his escape: He fashions a rope on the miniature spinning wheel. Years in the making, the rope is finished in true fairy-tale fashion, in time for rescue by good friends Ben, Naomi, and Dennis. The ending is a bit too conveniently Dickens, though we are promised a good sequel when Flagg vanishes.

We're not sure who owns the "good" in this story: "The Church of the Gods" is the community religion; The "white" resembles the modern-day "Force." King admits he doesn't know his sources—whether

luck, fate, or "those gods." However, good is the hands-down winner—
and that good always resides in the soul of a kind and loyal youth.

Good-bye and Keep Cold, by Jenny Davis (Watts/Orchard/Richard Jackson, 1987)

When the mine explodes, Edda's father dies. Though buried, his secrets
are just coming to light: He slept with Mama's best friend and is posthu-
mously divorced. The man responsible for the explosion takes up with
her mother. Well, maybe religion would help—no, it's superficial and
won't stand the weight of forgiveness.

Edda takes her fatherless brother through childhood with the help of
"Banker," an aging relative. He helps stabilize the family with his rich
profanities and gentle wisdom—and keeps memories alive by quoting
her father's proverbs. When Mama's dismissed lover marries, his little
handicapped baby appears one day on Mama's doorstep and is joyfully
raised by Edda, Jimmy and Mama.

The mother is warm, wise, vulnerable, and funny, making a life for her
family from the ashes of tragedy and betrayal. She begs Edda not to have
sex until she finishes high school. Edda obeys, waiting until college.

Edda wonders if her friend is right: "Everybody has to raise their
parents." Edda did the best she could with hers.

Greencastle, by Lloyd Kropp (Freundlich/Schribner, 1986)

It's small-town 1950s and Roger Cornell has some interesting friends—
a fantasy Martian, a melancholy genius who builds time machines, three
juvenile Egyptologists, and an anti-social bookstore owner.

The comic side of this story can't slow the speeding train of a boy's
dashed adolescent dreams. One by one, authority figures strip him of
whatever esteem is left to pubescent boys.

Increasingly Roger's slightly off-beat forays—the secret "Denizens of
the Sacred Crypt" meetings—and his friendship with Pangborn, the bookstore owner, earn him a spot of terrible recognition in the school, the "Concerned Mothers" meetings, and the ministerial association—all of whom
are out to protect America's youth from dirty books and communism.

Roger's rage is compounded when an unfeeling teacher triggers friend
Harry's suicide. Pangborn comes to the rescue in a last-ditch soap box
oration and puts to shame those people who seek to protect their youth

from unsavory activities and printed material. This is a boy-against-society story in the tradition of *The Catcher in the Rye* and *The Dead Poets Society.*

Invincible Summer, by Jean Ferris (Farrar/Straus/Giroux, 1987)

Seventeen-year-old Robin's farm days are filled with sunshine, until the doctor's pronouncement: she has leukemia.

Grandmother Libby's wisdom and caring can't be everything for Robin, and the pastor who looks like the Rev. Hamster is less than useful. It's not until she meets Rick that hope returns. Rick has leukemia too, so they encourage and cajole through the rough spots. Soon, friendship turns to love. Since Robin doesn't want to die a virgin, the two culminate their friendship in a hotel room. When Rick dies, and it looks as if Robin might live, she is again filled with despair.

Grandma comes to the rescue, helping Robin devise eternal words of wisdom: "The worst was that she would die. If death was the end, it was eternal sleep. If it was not, then she would be with Rick. There was nothing to worry about."

The author is skillful, and it's believable.

I Only Made Up the Roses, by Barbara Ann Porte (Greenwillow, 1987)

When Grandpa dies, the minister says, "He shall overcome the world." We're not sure whether this refers to Grandpa, but Cydra takes no chances: With pen in hand she brings Grandpa alive again.

When her white mother remarries, Cyd inherits a sensitive, educated black family. This diary paints the family portrait, face by face. Filled with ancestral triumphs and humorous stories, this book also adds black history lessons and challenges alleged female and black stereotypes.

Filled with love and Cydra's adolescent wisdom, we get a fresh—if pedagogic—glimpse into a loving black family.

Permanent Connections, by Sue Ellen Bridgers (Harper and Row, 1987)

Rob Dickson is angry—at his parents, at school, at the odd assortment of southern relatives he's sent to help, like Coralee, who fears the whole outdoors, and Grandpa, who is snippy and bedridden.

Rob's anger doesn't melt easily—a down-home diet of country folk is too tame after a life of rock music, drugs, and women—his steady fare back home. Little by little, Bridgers shuttles Rob through the loom of family anecdotes and tradition. Poised, intelligent classmate Ellery makes him all the more determined to prove how wicked he really is. Their friendship leads to lovemaking, making Ellery unsure, and Rob restless.

Things get sticky when his foolhardiness nearly kills Grandpa, and he's arrested for drug possession. Rob meets a minister who suggests he pray—to that something way down inside him.

Though Rob is guilty, the drug charges are dropped, and he has new respect for his father's commitment to free him.

Suddenly, life in his new school is "do-able," Ellery is back on the scene, and that weird extended family isn't so bad after all.

Rich in Love, by Josephine Humphreys (Viking/Penguin, 1987)

In coastal South Carolina, seventeen-year-old Lucille finishes reading her mother's farewell note and begins to parent her child-like father, who's lost his driver's license and will to live.

But Dad falls in love with the hairdresser—and steals away on the riding mower. Lucille's mothering problems compound when high-strung sister Rae comes home married and pregnant. It doesn't help that Lucille's boyfriend Wayne is always after her to have sex.

Providing equilibrium is wise, black friend Rhody.

Lucille's not prepared for the all-consuming love she feels for her brother-in-law, and this is the boost she needs to finally say "yes" to boyfriend Wayne on the pier one night. Numb with the ferocity of her feelings, she comes in the house and makes love again with her true love, her brother-in-law.

This story is stunningly crafted, with turns of phrase that would make Hemingway weep. But some may want to back away from what this author says so well.

The River in Winter, by David Small
(W. W. Norton and Co., 1987)

The river in winter is like a dried-up chocolate pie. And Joe sees with his heart, which is dying.

He can't forget his past—with a silly mother, runaway father, and abusive stepfather. He can't make a future—with its formidable rules, oppressive schools, and bad cops. He tries a strange friendship with his irascible, smelly grandfather, the part-time doctor. After remaking Grandpa into the man he once was, he meets Kathleen, the pristine judge's daughter.

Like a predictable, slow-paced nightmare, we know Joe can't survive. The lake's dreamlike peace is shattered by a bullet which kills Grandfather and the hope of justice. Aching passion and lovemaking for Kathleen can't survive either. Fate is out to get Joe, and under the frequently profane and skilled writing of David Small, it happens with horrifying certainty.

5

Don't Yell "Censor" In a Quiet Library

There's a national call to battle. The call is *"Censorship!"* But what a battle!

We can't tell whether the call is to "Censor!" or to clobber the censors. Woe to the bystander who strays onto the battlefield.

Because both sides are heavily armed: with half-truths, innuendo, guilt by association, name-calling, righteous anger—and the First Amendment.

You've Been Drafted!

If you don't know which army you're in, consult this battalion roster. Very likely you've been recruited.

You're Labeled a Right-Wing Fundamentalist Anti-Intellectual:

- If you ask for book removal from public libraries.
- If you challenge books because of sexual content, profanity, religious views, or lack of patriotism.
- If you're a parent who questions book content.
- If you're a minister who questions book content.
- If you're a school board member who questions curriculum.
- If you question a child's ability to handle any subject at any age.

- If you challenge an entire textbook system in its use of secular humanism, its omission of religious historical fact, or its inclusion of valueless decision-making, regardless of whether state law mandates such critique.

- If you accuse a librarian of censorship.

- If you withhold any book from your child.

- If you call anyone a "secular humanist."

You're Labeled a Left-Wing Liberal Humanist:

- If you represent the regular Media.

- If you uphold a child's right to read anything at any age.

- If you use "separation of church and state" interchangeably with "First Amendment rights."

- If you uphold a school system's right to omit religious historical fact.

- If you label a librarian's choices "selection," and other book challenges "censorship."

- If you crusade for balanced feminist or minorities-oriented library reading material.

- If you call anyone a "fundamentalist."

These labels aren't accurate. They aren't fair. *But it helps to know how the other side sees you.* And don't expect the two sides to agree on anything, or if they do, that it will be reported. What you can expect is that both sides will relish the anger which keeps them going.

So it was surprising to find fourteen national religious and educational groups actually agreeing on what to do about religion in the school. Yes, the National Education Association, the National Association of Evangelicals, and twelve other groups agreed that "study about religion in public schools, when done properly, is both constitutionally permissible and educationally sound."[1]

That's what lots of conservative parents have said for over thirteen years, a period which the American Library Association says marks dramatic increase in public school book challenges, both textbook and fiction. Indeed, most of these parents' "challenges" say there's a state "religion" in texts—and it isn't theirs!

But this combined report must not have found its way through both liberal and conservative echelons, because modern "ideological challenges" are still called "censorship" by most liberal organizations like the ACLU, People for the American Way, the National Education Association, mainstream media, and the American Library Association.

Groups like Concerned Women for America, Focus on the Family, Eagle Forum, and the National Legal Foundation say not all these challenges are censorship: some are "exercises of fundamental rights."

Cal Thomas in *Book Burning* says there's a growing shift in the public library and school-book selection process: Publishers, editors, librarians, teachers, and many media sources and their supporting professional organizations frequently dismiss or completely ignore Christian themes. This dismissal keeps Christian best-sellers off the *New York Times* list, in a tiny "religion" section in bookstores, and out of library reviews.

So, yes, parents challenge. They object. But the objection isn't to *themes* of violence, sex, and abortion—but to the *value-system* in which they're entrenched.

Not to be outflanked, People for the American Way say "would-be censors" want to restrict other kids' freedoms—not just their own kids'. They say these would-be censors want to put the lid on *all kids'* knowledge of basic sex education, like using condoms for AIDS prevention. PFAW

"So, yes, parents challenge. They object. But the objection isn't to themes of violence, sex, and abortion—but to the value-system in which they're entrenched."

---

says forty-two states fielded curriculum challenges in 1988–1989. By the final report of *Attacks on the Freedom to Learn*, these "challenges" became "censorship" or "ideological attacks."[2] So if you're talking censorship, you have to ask some serious questions: Who's doing it? What's the motive? and Why can educators do it, but not parents?

Establishment? Or Free Exercise?

Both sides of the censorship battle use the First Amendment for gun-powder: They just load different caliber guns and aim from opposite directions. Just what is that explosive little amendment that's brought life-changing decisions for two hundred years?

> *Bill of Rights, First Amendment (1791):* Congress shall make no law respecting an establishment of religion, or prohibiting the free exercise thereof; or abridging the freedom of speech, or of the press; or the right of the people peaceably to assemble, and to petition the Government for a redress of grievances.

The Constitution framers knew censorship firsthand. Most had fled "established" religious governments. They wanted none of that. But neither did they want their new government quashing religious expression.

This First Amendment took weeks to forge and two years to ratify. Now, for the sake of space, it's further amended to fit every-day speech. Now it's the "establishment clause" or "separation of church and state." These neat phrases, repeated year after year, become our sole memory of the Bill of Rights. Even well-educated Christians have described the First Amendment as "the separation of church and state amendment" or even "freedom *from* religion"!

The First Amendment's Balance Mechanism

"Establishment clause" standing out there all by itself isn't balanced. Fear of "*establishment*" sends us scrambling to snuff out every breath of spirituality: Fear of *establishment* banishes a child's voluntary schoolground prayers and the right to give his testimony in a valedictory address or classroom speech.

Was it fear that prompted the otherwise knowledgeable *Children and Books*, a major library college text shaping today's teachers, to tuck tail and say, "Since there can no longer be any exposure to religious literature in the public schools, such books become the exclusive responsibility of churches and homes"?[3]

But look at the rest of this textbook. In its "Regional and Religious Minorities" section, the author praises *All-of-a-Kind Family* (1951, Sydney Taylor) with, "A pleasanter emissary for Jewish culture, religious piety, and family love than (this) entertaining and heart-warming book could hardly be found."[4] Amish and Quaker stories are also tucked into this "Regional and Religious Minorities" section. We come to the chilling conclusion: *traditional, mainstream Christianity* can't have "exposure" in the public schools—all other religions can!

"Separation of church and state" is negative too. In fact, it doesn't even appear in our Constitution. It was Thomas Jefferson's private idea—in a letter to his nephew! One wishes he hadn't been so handy at metaphors: the phrase stuck, and now a private group with the same name: "Americans United for Separation of Church and State" has done its work well—most Americans think the phrase is sacredly preserved in the Bill of Rights. If our Constitution framers had intended true separation, they wouldn't have installed a Senate chaplain or minted "In God We Trust" on American coins.

Societies are shaped by word sculptors: What would the course of our history have been if, instead of parroting *the establishment clause* year after year, we'd said, *the free exercise clause?* This continual mouthing of "establishment" gives rise to such religion phobia that we "trust our kids" to sift through outrageous profanities, yet deny them a thirty-second graduation prayer because they're too "impressionable."

Scholar Richard John Neuhaus gives us a lesson in how to read the Bill of Rights: The negative "Establishment Clause" came first for this reason—to *ensure* religious freedom in the "Free Exercise" clause![5]

Plato Started It

Censorship isn't new. History texts gloss over Plato's call for government book bans. Plato feared for his "perfect society" and "impressionable" youth. Who should hold the highest government office? The Minister of Education, said Plato in *Laws*.[6] Keep the word "impressionable" well in mind: It's always the "official" reason to toss out Christian fiction and after-school religious groups.

But simply *talking* about censorship—or a writer's ideas—isn't censorship, no matter how vehemently we may express ourselves. The First Amendment protects dissenting ideas, too, giving us, if the mighty pen fails, the right to "petition the Government for redress of grievances." It isn't "censorship" to challenge "appropriate" reading materials. After all, the National Education Association does it: When it comes to "women's rights" their committee reports call for "promot[ion of] methods, such as textbook evaluation and revision, for inclusive curricula and instructional delivery systems which ensure equity in education."[7]

And as much as we deplore Anthony Comstock's fire-breathing vice raids and book burnings of 1906 to 1914, he slashed and burned with federal statute blessing.[8] If you want to change laws like this, do it with pen and voice and vote.

Do Librarians Censor?

Government agents aren't the only ones who censor. Librarians have always fought the urge to align their collections with personal preference. Who can be totally objective? Don't we come to our jobs with a lifetime of biases and opinions? Couple this with low budgets and time constraints, and you have a fragile bunch of librarians who are just like everybody else: fallible.

Library imbalance might happen this way:

In a small town, a librarian stacks the collection with personal favorites. She doesn't realize her anti-religious bias and likes to say she's a "forward thinker," not a censor. But other "thinkers" (who've run "forward" in another direction) challenge the library and are tapped by wire services as "dangerous fundamentalists" and by conservative presses as "concerned parents."

In another town, a conservative librarian reflects the community bent and leans another way. But in this case citizens say he's created ethnic and feminist imbalance. These alert citizens will be labeled "brave crusaders" or "dangerously liberal," depending on your news source.

How do we keep such things from happening?

When All Else Fails, Issue Guidelines

But I challenge you to show me completely objective guidelines: They reflect the people who wrote them. They're interpreted by those who use them. And if they're worded cleverly enough and given enough time, they'll be engraved on stone.

Each state's association of school boards issues guidelines for everything from sewer lines to teacher salaries. Walk into your local school board office and ask for this year's "education guidelines." You won't have time to read anything else all year. Buried in this morass is a few

---

"It isn't 'censorship' to challenge 'appropriate' reading materials. After all, the National Education Association does it."

---

pages—or a booklet—on "book content challenges." It's nice to have something to show the public when censors darken the door. Each state has one.

Iowa's school board member "Guide" says those with "specialized knowledge" should select texts.[9] Iowa's Association also encourages specific, open communication with parents, which is something good to have in mind when you encourage specific, open communication with the school board.[10]

New York State's "Textbook Selection" position paper devotes a whole chapter to "Parental Involvement." You'd expect a few breezy pages on parent-teacher cooperation. Instead, it's a fear-racked chapter on parent-phobia—"vocal" parents, parents who "censor," parents "with specific agendas," parents who might have "narrow views," parents who want their children to "opt out completely from common learnings."[11]

This position paper says it's dangerous to let citizens impact text selection, for (parents) could "impose their views" in court and "challenge directly the philosophy and goals of public education."[12]

New York's position paper says their boards champion "diverse views" and imply that Alabama parents in the famous "secular humanism" case do not.

How About Parental Input Before the Guidelines?

Twenty-one states allow citizen input *before* textbook purchase. Mel and Norma Gabler obey the Texas citizen-input law and respond with newsletters and books. They expose publisher omissions in history and literature and the lack of diversity in religious viewpoints. They challenge non-abstinence sex education. More than fifteen thousand public and private citizens hear from the Gablers; media sources estimate upwards of 50 percent of all textbook challenges result from Gabler newsletters. Texas is a gargantuan textbook consumer: Publishers gauge the country's ideological climate by Texas, California, and New York.

Those who don't agree with the Gablers cite their reports as dangerous, radical, right-wing fundamentalist, and worse.

What's so dangerous about doing business the American way? Can't I give my opinion and persuade others by thorough research? The Gablers are simple consumers in the supposedly competitive business of public education.

No doubt this "research" is contrary to what some education masters want to hear. Since when is research dangerous and self-expression against the law? To silence these reports would shoot a far more ragged hole through the First Amendment than an orderly parental book challenge.

Onalee McGraw, formerly of the Heritage Foundation says, "Perhaps the liberal cultural arbiters are concerned about the influence 'from the right' because they recall how readily the textbook publishers acceded to demands from the left in the past."[13]

Indeed, the New York School Board "position paper" concedes that such liberal pressures have changed texts just as often as have conservative ones. Over the past twenty years, they say, pictures of little girls with dolls were replaced by women doctors and truck drivers, while illustrations now show men out of their offices and in less traditional roles. Minority stereotypes were also removed.[14] Because 90 percent of all librarians are now women, it would be hard to prove that such feminist bias does not exist.

Voices like McGraw's are seldom heard because they document the embarrassing reality that publishers, librarians, and reviewers do their own "pre-emptive" or "variable" censoring. With thousands of new books vying for shelf space each year, this constitutes a staggering *millions* of books subjected to such pre-emptive "selection."

Parents with the legal mandate to put kids in school also have the legal right to question and impact their school's curriculum selection—whether through simple school board vote or written petition and a voice on the board's docket.

Curiously, parents who rail at apple producers about pesticides in baby food are courageous "Davids" against corporate "Goliaths." Parents who speak out for their child's mental and moral development are candidates for treason.

"Since when is research dangerous and self-expression against the law? To silence these reports would shoot a far more ragged hole through the First Amendment than an orderly parental book challenge."

The Library "Bill of Rights"

To their credit, the private American Library Association responds to in-house censorship attempts with updated versions of the 1939 Library Bill of Rights. The 1930s librarians crusaded for their young patrons' morals, and the ALA feared self-censorship.[15] With a title like "Library Bill of Rights," and fifty years of entrenchment, these guidelines begin to sound like a piece of the United States Constitution and some of its users like Supreme Court Justices.

When the Grinnell, Iowa school board put *Slaughterhouse-Five* and *A Hero Ain't Nothin' But a Sandwich* on hold in 1977, the librarian told the media that two administrators approved book purchase on the face value of specially designed reviews. The librarian "said there are books and magazines she would not have in the library, but 'We call it select rather than censor.'"[16]

It's "select, not censor" that puts school boards above parents, and librarians behind a professional fortress. Few dare storm the gates.

Though the Library Bill of Rights is a remarkable piece of work—providing diversity, balance, respect for all religions, peoples, and ideas—this "bill" filters through real people. It isn't surprising when the finished product is imbalance or anger.

Righteous Anger, or Forgiveness?

Unfortunately, in the super-charged battle for our children, anger is the uniform that makes both armies look most like the enemy. Nothing scoots us to phone or typewriter quicker than anger. "Man's anger does not promote God's righteousness" (James 1:20, RSV), but it sure gets us to the polls.

Can we be just as motivated by Christ's forgiveness and love? Do we dare use it when dealing with the school system?

In our forty-five fiction books, themes of grudging acceptance replaced true forgiveness; and time—that solid scapegoat for evolution's folly—was the healer: worse, it became the clever imitation of Christ's model.

Copying this type of forgiveness won't solve the deeper problems behind censorship: Nothing but real forgiveness based on truth brings warring armies to the peace table.

Over six hundred Alabama parents and teachers tried reasoning and forgiveness, but they finally took their textbook challenge to court. The now-famous Alabama secular humanism case of 1987 still echoes through anti-censorship books and conservative presses, getting a fair trial in neither.

The Alabama "censorship" case didn't begin with textbooks. It began in 1982 when a Mobile father of three took his county's schools to court for allowing prayer and religious observances. An opposing father "requested alternate relief"—saying that if Christian observances went out the school window, secular humanism must follow.

By the time the reorganized case went to trial, parents who'd opposed father number 1 now challenged whole textbook series as "secular humanism." More than six hundred parents and teachers were now the plaintiffs, and the Mobile County School system the defendant. This was the case: Do Mobile County textbooks promote secular humanism, and is secular humanism a religion?

Five years after that first challenge, the District Court gave a decision: Judge Brevard Hand declared secular humanism a religion in 1987 and ordered the questionable texts *be used only when opposing viewpoints could be taught at the same time.*

Both liberals and conservatives leave out important facts when they tell this story.

"It's 'select, not censor' that puts school boards above parents, and librarians behind a professional fortress. Few dare storm the gates."

Liberals almost always call the six hundred plaintiffs "fundamentalists," when in fact they represent a variety of backgrounds and theistic religions. Both liberal and conservative presses were embarrassed with a "fundamentalist" teacher's testimony because it didn't fit their formula: she said the so-called humanistic texts *were* usable—because she could supplement them with her own traditional philosophy.[17]

Absolute Breakdown in Morality

But most embarrassing of all for the liberals is the court testimony by one of humanism's gurus, Paul Kurtz. Professor of Philosophy at the State University of New York at Buffalo, and one of the signers of Humanist Manifesto II, he is well known for statements like "We deplore efforts to look outside nature for salvation, or trying to explain the world in supernatural terms."[18]

But he'd read the texts in the Alabama case and, as a principal witness for the *schools,* said he agreed with the *parents* in some respects— "If the curriculum in these aspects were followed by the students, it would lead to *an absolute breakdown in morality in society* [emphasis mine]. . . . such teachings deny to the educational process what is known as critical thinking."[19]

Is Humanism a Religion?

Humanist Paul Kurtz himself testified that secular humanism is a religion. "Humanism is a philosophical, religious and moral point of view as old as civilization itself."[20] Corliss Lamont, a household name to the humanism movement, concurs. He promotes a "humanist burial service" for true believers.[21] Judge Hand agreed that humanism lines up with all major definitions of religion:

Humanism has structured groups that proselytize and preach. Humanists conduct seminars and retreats. Humanism has leaders, alive and deceased. Humanism makes statements based on "faith" assumptions. Humanism defines the nature of the Universe.[22]

Alabama court witnesses gave page after page of documented evidence showing:

- Textbooks demean Judeo-Christian values.

- Teachers can't teach right or wrong.

- Teachers can't teach Evolution's opposing theories or teach beliefs contrary to celebrating Halloween.

- "The religion of secular humanism" (a definition the Appeals Court let stand) has completely taken over the curriculum.

The six hundred litigants said they weren't "out to get the books." Their motive was to document in court that Alabama textbooks promote *one* religion as more favorable than another.

They say they're not against controversial subjects: The question isn't whether to ban "everything from divorce to evolution," as People for the American Way claim.[23] The question is whether to allow equal time for *all* views on subjects from divorce to evolution.

"A Dangerous Doctrine?"

Trust Your Children, a publication by People for the American Way, says the Alabama trial exposes a dangerous doctrine, one "that seeks to protect [the litigants'] children, and ultimately all children, from being exposed to ideas with which they disagree. [The litigants'] argument can be boiled down to this: That unless our public schools teach their religious dogma, we are undermining the religious faith of their children, and violating their constitutional rights."[24]

But the Alabama parents didn't oppose diversity; they objected to one religion taking over, in clear violation of the "establishment clause." They "are not asking that their beliefs be imposed on anyone, just the opposite. [But] taxpayers, including themselves, should not be forced to support a system that works against their efforts to pass on their faith to their children."[25]

Church of the Public School

Dr. William Coulson, Professor of Psychology and Education at the United States International University in 1987, summarized in court the Alabama textbooks' impact: Children who have been raised and educated in the schools over the last twenty years or so are in special jeopardy because this relativism which has been espoused has become the church of the public school.[26]

Coulson made a public apology in 1989 for joining Carl Rogers twenty years ago to foist an experimental value-free program on some California Catholic schools.

Coulson says it was a "person-centered" approach, inverting reasoning with feelings. Rogers, too, confessed that the original psycho-therapeutic aim of the program was to invert reason with feelings. Both Coulson and Rogers gave up the project early in the game, but the R. J. Reynolds family (of Reynolds tobacco) funded the original pilot. They still promote the underlying philosophy in a multi-million dollar "Helping Youth Decide" program. Coulson says this program fosters tobacco use because kids aren't told what's right and wrong.[27]

Carl Rogers gave up the original project, regretting its impact until his death in 1990. But the philosophy of this "quiet revolutionary" on the cutting edge of the humanist movement continues to cast its "me-centered" bread upon the waters, never mind that it returns moldy. We are fooled into thinking its greenly tinged edges are "the sprouting green of new life."[28]

This "sprouting green" wilts for all who use it. But because Rogers' goal was process-oriented, rather than product-oriented, an entire generation of Americans is eternally fooled into searching for "the real me" and is scared witless when it is found in all its naked, powerless glory.[29] Short, interchangeable personal relationships, no definite life answers, and no one to lean on except self—this is enough to make some of these Rogerian converts run screaming into the night. What do they do in the cold, value-free night? They begin again: new relationships, new truth—and a basic fear of toppling Rogers from his ill-placed pedestal. (Carl Rogers, says Coulson, is more widely accepted as *the* humanistic psychologist, surpassing even Sigmund Freud and B. F. Skinner.)[30]

A Vacuum of Values

Prayer was booted out of public schools in 1963, and because officials ran scared, all things religious soon followed. "Relevance" swiftly flew in on silent wings. Following closely behind this new realism was a polyglot of values clarification, self-esteem pilots, and me-centered problem-solvers. As early as 1967 a seventh-grade Scott, Foresman reader shows us the Gutenberg press but not its greatest masterpiece: the Gutenberg Bible.[31] It brings to life a Roman girl in the time of Herod Antipas, but omits Jews and Jesus.[32] Author Rosemary Sutcliff talks of writers being "lantern bearers" for "responsive" young people, but who gets to choose the "lantern"?[33]

What's Relevant?

Former English teacher Jeff Taylor remembers how quickly the classics disappeared from West Virginia middle school "readers" when he taught language arts for eight years in the 1980s. In a move for "relevance," the old was out, the new was in. Sherlock Holmes was ditched in favor of a Hispanic theme; Robert Frost by inner city stories. "There seemed to be a tokenism quota system at the expense of enduring literature."[34]

Ravitch and Finn cite this new "relevance" as one of the reasons seventeen-year-olds no longer score big on classic literature.[35]

By 1984, when a Congressional committee heard hundreds of coast to coast "mind abuse" complaints from angry and frightened parents, the "values" mechanism was so firmly entrenched in public schools that Congress passed a special bill to *enforce* an act already permitting parents access to their children's curriculum. "Values" became the watchword of the 1980s, and many school systems scrambled to untangle the mess which a Kids-know-best education had given our youth.

Many schools, texts, and teachers claim they don't teach values. But aside from math and some technical science, values can't be scraped off the top of social sciences like so much burnt toast. It's not a question of *some* values or *no* values. It's a question of *my* values or *your* values. Or, in the true modern tradition: my values *and* your values.

Whose Values?

While substitute teaching on team-teaching days I have watched in silent gratitude while skillful teachers impart strong, traditional values. I have come into classrooms delighted to see a Thomas Jefferson quote advis-

---

"Values can't be scraped off the top of social sciences like so much burnt toast. It's not a question of some values or no values. It's a question of my values or your values. Or, in the true modern tradition: my values and your values."

---

ing kids to "obey their parents." I've sat quietly in a corner as the teacher forbids his class to make rude remarks to other students. One wishes such teachers were in every classroom.

But which values would you say are being taught in classrooms where some instructors regularly teach meditation, psychology "dream trips," and numerology exercises?

It truly is a question of *whose* values!

Try making a "no values" guide for school library selection or anti-censorship. It can't be done. Note the super-charged "value" words in these quotes:

If the schools had "clear and comprehensible curricular objectives and chose books to support them, administrators would be in a better position to argue the merits of . . . textbook selections."[36]

We simply ask that libraries show the same sensitivity to the feelings of (those of) traditional morality that has generally been shown to blacks in the context of materials selection.[37]

Judy Blume: "The longer I'm a parent, the less I'm sure of what's right and what's wrong. Anyone who's too sure of himself is the one I doubt."[38]

A trial should be held to determine if the School Board's action had the intention of stifling unpopular ideas.[39]

But sometimes a book is bought that we're sorry about.[40]

But a classic, once you penetrate it, lifts you up *high!*[41]

Read for information, read for pleasure, read for inspiration.[42]

Contrary to what some of the community reformers think, the very authors they are trying to abolish may well be their salvation and their hope.[43]

The author should make a point.[44]

Young people are so much more sophisticated today that "we would be shortchanging them to limit the possibilities they have access to."[45]

And that's where the difference between randomly picking and deliberately choosing—discerning good books from dull books—comes in.[46]

It's an anachronism—books like that which were perfectly acceptable years ago just don't fit into modern life.[47]

Nancy (Drew) . . . communicates an important set of values to her young readers.[48]

If your get kids interested in reading books—no matter what sort— eventually they will go on to grander literature by themselves.[49]

One person's selection is another person's censorship.[50]

Wherever possible, at least two favorable reviews from reputable sources will be required . . . before ordering a title.[51]

The accusations of local cranks seldom prevail when the library's operations are based on clearcut and timely procedures that reflect thorough research, sound judgment, and careful planning.[52]

Polarized or Pluralized?

The above authors thought we'd know exactly what they meant by their "value" words. Did they think our values stem from the mistaken notion of a "kinder, gentler nation"? For this "kindness" we're banking on a left-over value system—a notion that we're a Judeo-Christian nation. Some argue that we're a pluralistic society and a "post-Christian" nation. A "kinder, gentler nation" may now rest on the shifting quicksand of a valueless, "me-first" generation.

The typical public school approach is to take every cultural and ethical system dotting the world's shores, mix them up in a bucket, and leave it to our kids to ladle out "what's best for them." Whether individual teachers *want to* reflect community values is often beside the point—textbooks and the valueless curriculum of the last twenty years often sidestep the teacher. In most sex-education manuals, for instance, teachers are instructed to omit such value words as "marriage" so they will not "offend" those children whose parents and/or guardians aren't married! Most administrators feel pressured to uphold this policy. AIDS curriculum guidelines specifically direct teachers NOT to share their values.

It's hard for kids to ladle something meaningful from such a homogenized bucket. More recently, that bucket has sprouted leaks: Little by little, vital pieces of religious history, traditional values, and the classics have been removed. Now much that's left is solid, sticky goo. Some say that goo is "secular humanism," "New Age," or "Values-Free." And they want it put in its proper place—as only one of many ideas. That's ideal "pluralism."

But that's not what we have in American public schools.

Pluralism is really polarization.

Here's why: As much as we yearn to get Judeo-Christian traditionists and secular humanists to the peace table, it seldom happens.

Indeed, some say it *can't* happen because *both come to the peace table with different rules.* When neither side compromises, the peace accords disperse amidst shouting and raving.

These two sets of rules aren't apparent at first, because both secular humanism and Judeo-Christian traditionists claim some common values: both shout for individual worth. Both prize freedom. Both have a code of ethics. Both want the best for their children and are willing to pay for it.

So what's the problem?

We don't disagree about the good things we prize—just about where they come from!

What Secular Humanists Believe

Secular humanists say God doesn't intervene in our affairs. They say the church is a crumbling institution, and the sooner it's replaced the better.

In fact, there are so many different kinds of humanists—the one thing many of them *do* agree on is their abhorrence of theistic religion (except for so-called "religious" humanists, who have a boot in both camps).

So where do humanists say we get individual worth, freedom, and ethics?

They say we get it from ourselves. We evolved from nothing, responsible to nothing. We're still evolving. Time is our best friend—the more we have, the better we get at things like freedom, worth, and ethics. The humanist's freedom is based on a show of hands: it's what *you* think about it. It's what *I* think about it. Kids can decide at any age "what's best for *me*." We learn from each other and gain worth from self-motivated accomplishments. Everything is relative. Nothing is *absolutely* true. Except, of course, that it is *absolutely* true there are no absolutes.

What Judeo-Christians Believe

And where does the Judeo-Christian get freedom, individual worth and ethics? He says it comes from a loving God who is personally involved in Creation. Though interpretations vary by sect, all these folks claim a basic Book of Absolutes written by God Himself.

When Isaiah said, "Come, let us reason together" (Isaiah 1:18), he pulled the humanists along in hopeful fashion. In fact, humanists often quote this passage with relish.

It's Isaiah's next phrase (*Says the Lord!*, 1:18) that divides secular humanists from theists. Even harder for humanists to swallow is the following pardon—"Though your sins are like scarlet, they shall be as white as snow." (Isaiah 1:18, RSV). This idea of sin and its need for forgiveness separates the humanist from the Judeo-Christian as surely as oil separates from water.

ta. ta. ta.

In short, humanists claim there are absolutely no absolutes, and Judeo-Christian traditionists claim divine absolutes. With that kind of disparity, it would be hard to agree on things like teacher-student ratios or affirmative action, much less a system for choosing K-12 curriculum! What makes it even stickier is that only about 10 percent of parents and teachers see the disparity. The other 90 percent go about their quiet business of trying to raise decent human beings.

"In short, humanists claim there are absolutely no absolutes, and Judeo-Christian traditionists claim divine absolutes."

On behalf of these future "decent human beings," I suggest a new battle: a battle to control anger, engage in quiet, long-term diplomacy, and render to Caesar only that which is his.

6

What You Can Do

I can't imagine your reading this book without wanting to do some-thing. Either you think I'm an outrageous censor, or you believe in research. It's time to ask: "What should I do about my kids' books?" You can almost smell sulphur burning in the muskets and have gone to the attic to dust off the uniform.

But before you rush out the door with wrinkled khakis and outdated manuals, please count the cost.

Whatever you choose to do will be a spiritual battle. It will be long and costly. It won't be over in one month or six. We gave our children, our schools, and our rights to the state over a period of sixty years. We won't get them back in sixty days.

It took twenty-four years to put our three children through thirteen schools. I've subbed or taught in five different school districts. I've made a lot of mistakes, and I've done a lot of things right. Here's what I suggest after this hands-on experience:

- Dress for battle.

- Know your reason for reading. What's "good literature"?

- Know your rights from Constitution to classroom.

- Know your responsibilities—from school involvement to teaching "good" literature. Keep current—with liberal *and* conservative sources.

- Inspire others—for encouragement and restraint.

- Have a ten-year goal.

- Act.

Dress for Battle

What does today's parent activist wear? Anger. Let's face it: Anger is fun. Moral crusades start with a bang, then fizzle. That's because they're based on outrage. We feed on the righteous indignation of *our* hurt, *our* outrage, *our* rights! The cloak of anger isn't becoming. It won't get me what I want. Instead I need two things: spiritual preparation and a long-range strategy.

Paul sent good advice to the Church in ancient Ephesus. The plan still works! His battle dress is good for skirmish or full-scale war. That's because his Smithsonian-looking battle gear is just as powerful today as it was two thousand years ago. In fact, it's the *only* thing that works. But I need to wear every piece: it won't do any good hanging in the closet!

> But to do this, you will need the strong belt of truth and the breast-plate of God's approval. Wear shoes that are able to speed you on as you preach the Good News of peace with God. In every battle you will need faith as your shield to stop the fiery arrows aimed at you by Satan. And you will need the helmet of salvation and the sword of the Spirit—which is the Word of God. (Ephesians 6:14–17, TLB)

I ran for school board in 1990 on a strong curriculum-challenge platform. I was labeled and skewered. But never before or since have I been so at peace with God. This is all the more amazing when I remember how fear reduced me to a quivering heap one week before the filing deadline. But once committed, and with fifty friends who began to pray, that shield of faith protected me in a way I'd read about, but never experienced. With all that good armor in place, even the hard questions were answerable.

With *your* armor in place, I suggest you put those hard questions where they belong—with the family.

What Is My Family Definition of Good Literature?

You know what the good stuff is. You know what you want your kids to read. Or do you? An English professor once asked for our "personal rubric" of good literature. He didn't tell us what good literature is: He *asked* his class of future teachers to make a personal definition.

What's your rubric? Do you want your child to read a personal-God-centered novel? Then know what you want that novel to do. Do you want that book to do nothing more than teach your child moral absolutes? Or perhaps you're offended at blatant preaching. Maybe you hold out for allegorical invitation—the fragrant beauty of a hidden secret inviting your child to know the love of God. If others push preachy books, and you don't want them—say so!

Do you want nuts-and-bolts, personal-God-centered answers to prejudice, abortion, suicide? You're the only one who knows your child well enough to define his needs. But in this area we can take a lesson

---

"The classics may have endured, but the ones currently taught in our schools are weak on godliness."

---

from Jesus Himself. He taught in parables, and He taught by example. Only the hard of heart needed negative preaching. Make your rubric as if it's of life and death importance to your teenager. It is!

Now, find the books—buy them, borrow them, scatter them all through the house. Ask your home-schooler friends what their kids read: By necessity they've researched this topic inside out. *Initiate* an answer to the current wisdom that says, "Leave your child alone and she'll pick good literature." And most important of all, let your children see you reading those books yourself.

Gladys Hunt's *Honey for a Child's Heart* (Zondervan, 1978) and Elizabeth Wilson's *Books Children Love* (Crossway, 1987) give detailed, thoughtful reviews of enduring youth literature, and insight on a child's need for beauty and truth. Some of their recommended books are hard to find; you may need an inter-library loan, or a trip to the Christian bookstore. One of the reasons Christian books aren't in the public library is that not enough people are brave enough or knowledgeable enough to ask for them. See chapter 8 for books we recommend.

If you want your child to read books that *aren't* centered on a personal God, you won't have trouble finding them. And you won't have to finish this chapter.

What about the classics? Aren't they just as good? I wanted to know. So I dusted off my classics and put them to the test. I had to agree with Bryce Christensen, associate editor of *Chronicles: A Magazine of American Culture*. The classics may have endured, but the ones currently taught in our schools are weak on godliness. Christensen studied the prayers of some of our most esteemed literary characters, like Holden Caulfield of *The Catcher in the Rye*. Says Christensen, "most of the literary prayers now studied at taxpayer expense are . . . ineffectual, incomplete, or ironic."[1]

Ask your city librarian for an American Library Association list of classics. Read them. If you don't like "classics," you're not "anti-literature." You're simply exercising your "academic freedom." It's time to ask why the *Des Moines Register* ran this story: "If *Grapes of Wrath* isn't taught in schools, it may disappear" (March 5, 1980). (The Bible isn't taught in public schools, and it hasn't disappeared.)

After you've worked through that personal definition, you can change from *reactor* to *initiator*.

How would you *react* to these two questions?

- "Do you really think you can protect your kids from the world?"

- "Don't you know that restricting a child's reading material is censorship?"

Before I developed my personal rubric, my *reaction* was bumbling and limp. Something like, "Well, uh, I guess you're right, but . . . Well—don't *you* think they should have help?"

I suggest that you *initiate*. Make the first statement! You can say things like:

"Kids need truth to arm themselves for the world. Current fiction isn't accurate statistically or morally."

And, "You say books can't harm kids? Then it would be just as true to say that books can't do them any good. I'm pushing them to read. So it makes sense to know *what* they're reading."

Recently, my husband described an explosive lunchroom conversation that was all *reacting* and no *initiating*. One of his co-workers described a steamy teen novel her daughter brought home from school. In a flash, another employee attacked her with rapier speed, accusing censorship and parental interference. Calming the storm with his usual tact,

---

"Your child's English teacher talks with your child—for a total of two thousand hours in thirteen years! Total strangers in the guise of fiction authors command up to six hundred hours a year of your child's time!"

Jerry was able to field the conversation to research findings (mine) and common sense (his). The mother and her co-worker were both armed—yes, but only *partially*. When dealing with an emotional issue like censorship, half-armed will get you dead in the water.

Once you've taken the offensive, you can do these things:

One: Promote Good Literature in Your Home

If you're not reading with your kids, read. Whereas 85 percent of all youth fiction is bought by public libraries, teen romances capture half the paperback market, and your teen girls can get them anywhere. Know what these romances say before your kids do. (The location of the hands on the cover will give you a clue about what's inside.) But before you give any fiction the heave-ho, read enough to ask your teen intelligent questions. *Then* if that book doesn't belong in your house, say so and stick with your rules. "Academic freedom" is not an iron clamp which keeps you from running your own home!

But not all lopsided books are threatening if kids can also read the opposing views—and if you can talk about them. After all, your child's English teacher talks with your child—for a total of two thousand hours in thirteen years! Total strangers in the guise of fiction authors command up to six hundred hours a year of your child's time! A word of caution here: Opposing views of many teens' problems will *not* be found in the school library. You will have to look elsewhere.

Two: Ask, "Why Is Literature Taught in School?"

Before 1970, literature was taught largely as an art form and to inspire students to appreciate "truth and beauty." It's a holdover from turn-of-the-century texts like *Baldwin's Readers* (circa 1897), which says sixth and seventh graders are "now prepared to devote more and more attention to literary criticism—that is, to the study of the peculiarities of style which distinguish any selection, the passages which are remarkable for their beauty, their truth. . . ."[2]

Not so today: *Literature is taught so students will find life's answers in good writing!* In most schools English literature belongs in the psychology or philosophy departments. Much of new fiction isn't even good writing! And if we compare it to *Baldwin's Readers* of one hundred years ago, it's an intellectual catastrophe. Beginning its trickle-down from the universities is the current literature-teaching fad of "reader response," which says you don't have to know what the author meant. Anything you "feel" is your response—and, you guessed it—nothing is right or wrong as long as you can defend it.

Wouldn't it be great if our public schools used the 1869 librarian of Congress' definition of a good book: "The true question to ask respecting a book, is, 'has it help'd any human soul?'"[3]

The rationale for much of today's book offerings seems to be, "Just get them to read!" With that kind of logic we should barrage the school cafeteria with candy bars and cake so we can "Just get them to eat!" Of *course* kids will eat the candy bars! Of *course* kids will go for occult and sexually explicit books!

Literature was once taught so kids would learn reading and writing. More and more, students are told, "Good stories answer your problems." So rampant is this thinking that many universities now give courses—or even majors—in *bibliotherapy,* in which a librarian or teacher is the modern therapist, and your child the patient. If fiction is therapy, teachers and librarians are facilitators for your child's mental health.

What Are My Rights?

What kind of facilitator should *I* be? Should I do anything about these promoted books?

What usually keeps parents from acting is simple ignorance. We've constructed our rights from a crazy quilt of school, media, the National Education Association, the conservative press, and our neighbor. Stitched with flimsy thread, that quilt of rights won't cover us for the simplest library challenge: The first rebuttal from teacher, administrator, or librarian sends us whimpering home.

But a word of caution: Demanding rights without carrying out responsibilities—and without a long-range plan—will put us in the same hot seat as the "definitive censor."

What Not to Do

If your child's library book runs contrary to all that you've tried to teach him at home, you could march to your school and demand its removal. That's instantly gratifying. And deadly. Even your best friend will call you a censor. Others will have choice names for you, too. But even if you don't fit this description, be prepared—sooner or later you'll get the label anyway. That's because censorship's current definition is based on what happens to two kinds of books: *books on the shelf*—which you don't dare take off. And *books that haven't made it to the public library*—which you haven't heard of.

This woman came in yelling. It doesn't matter whether you're logical or outrageous: if you have a question about library books, the stock description making the rounds is, "This woman (or man—usually a minister) came in yelling about that dirty book. . . ."

Their second remark about the supposed censor is "She didn't even read the book!" Or, "She didn't even finish the book!" (Keep this in mind if your book challenge makes it to the school board: chances are that not everyone on the board has finished the book).

"This woman" made five mistakes: She didn't finish the book. She didn't ask anyone else to read it with her. She didn't look at the whole book to determine literary merit. She didn't compare it with a statistical sampling of other library books. And—worst of all—she was "yelling." Ironically, the only thing that woman did right was to exercise her Constitutional prerogatives. Unfortunately, her lack of preparation erased all her good intentions.

Parent-school confrontations are painstakingly tallied by groups like People for the American Way. Each year a list of "censorship attempts or ideological attacks" is printed on slick paper to outrage the public. Because so many believe the half-truths and convoluted reasoning behind this research, anything you do to question books will be considered censorship. So arm yourself with hard answers for embarrassing questions. And be prepared to face the wrath of three well-heeled organizations (American Civil Liberties Union, People for the American Way, and the American Library Association) if you get to stage eight in your book challenge. They'll back their wrath with money and lawyers.

But most importantly: Be prepared to change your ways if you *are* wrong! On both sides of any conflict are people who don't want to admit mistakes. This self-preservation is what fuels tiny challenges all out of proportion. "This same attitude which was in Christ Jesus" (Philippians 2:5) is not the same attitude which many Christians like to drag into public fights.

Know Your History

If these forty-five books are a mirror image of public-school thought, we need to study this philosophy—and your rights.

Three hundred years ago, the Massachusetts Colony required formal instruction for settlements of over fifty families. But most schooling until the middle of the nineteenth century was some form of home instruction. Literacy rates were high—so why did we change? Horace Mann had a vision for public schools—and his one-man education army was the beginning of "modern" schooling. Samuel Blumenfeld documents the push for public education as an organized ploy of nineteenth-century secularists who wanted Christianity choked out of successful home schools.[4] They took the Constitution's uncertainties and rammed public education into America's machinery "for a public experiment." And there it lodged.

These secularists then pushed the states—one by one—to public education, with the last state falling into lockstep only sixty short years ago. In fact, it wasn't until the middle of this century that a federal department of education existed! Since then, the number of local school districts has declined at an alarming rate. From over a quarter of a million districts in 1932, we have distilled our parent-owned power into the hands of a mere sixteen thousand districts today. With population adjustment, that's *thirty times* fewer districts than sixty years ago![5] The National Education Association, the most powerful labor union in our country, wants to multiply this control, with their goal of federally-controlled teacher and school accreditation potentially sapping even more parent power. No wonder Chicago parents demanded a separate district for each school!

Loss of Real Power

Where does this leave our rights? Since 1932, our basic rights haven't changed as much as our *real power*. We go about band-aiding education with more money; by default we push educators into making all *our* decisions. We think the yellow school bus safely delivers kids from public school to state university or job market. If some state legislatures have their way with early childhood education, our kids will be on that yellow bus at age two!

Look at your state school power charts. Now read school documents. On paper, your local board has power. In reality, their directives come from the local superintendent or state department of education.

> *"Be prepared to change your ways if you are wrong! On both sides of any conflict are people who don't want to admit mistakes. This self-preservation is what fuels tiny challenges all out of proportion."*

We have abrogated our rights. And all without a struggle. What happened to the public school is our fault. Because we copped out of our responsibilities, we lost the power behind our rights. And we won't get it back without a fight.

Do You Remember Your Constitution?

While we've been nurturing kids and strengthening our moral and family base, others have been studying the U. S. Constitution. And their modern, radical interpretation isn't what we remember! Since school prayer toppled from grace in 1963, little-known court cases have dotted the national landscape, creating a matrix of legal precedents that have turned the First Amendment on its head. In many parts of the country, this is what The First Amendment looks like now:

You're breaking the law and "establishing religion":

- If you allow a student to deliver a commencement address which describes her personal relationship with God.

- If a teacher or student reads a Bible privately and silently in the classroom during free-reading time.

- If you allow two or three books of Bible stories in a classroom "mini" library.

- If you allow Bibles in the school library.

- If you allow commencement prayer.

You're allowing "freedom of speech":

- If you promote anti-American or anti-Christian speakers at your university without allowing equal time for opposing views.

- If you allow public school "academic freedom" for every social view except the Judeo-Christian one.

- If you allow slander against Judeo-Christian values but not against racial and ethnic minorities, homosexuals, handicaps, and women.

Study the Constitution! If you don't have a copy, buy one. If you have it, read it. We've allowed "experts" to read and interpret it for us. And when you're finished, read that "other" constitution—your state's. There's a jumbo education section just waiting for you to study. You'll find it at your public library.

What about the Ninth Amendment? Rarely quoted, it says plenty about your family's rights. "The enumeration in the Constitution, of certain rights, shall not be construed to deny or disparage others retained by the people." The "right to privacy" in birth control, abortion, and sexual activity is supposedly implied in this amendment.

The "Ninth" also spawned the Hatch Amendment of 1974 and 1978. This Amendment gives your child the privacy he should have had when "values clarification" gave his beliefs a mismatched fight in the public schools. But it took nationwide Congressional hearings in 1984 to prompt Congress to enact legislation just to enforce the Hatch Amendment!

Specifically called *The Federal Protection of Pupil Rights Act,* the Hatch Amendment gives parents legal access to all curriculum materials, and says your child can't

1. be subjected to psychological examination or treatment,
2. be required to reveal "political affiliations," "sexual behavior and attitudes," "mental and psychological problems potentially embarrassing to the student or his family,"
3. be asked for "critical appraisals" of behavior and attitudes of family members without the "prior written consent of the parent."[6]

The Pupil Protection Act is just vague enough to allow vastly different interpretations. Take "journal writing." This diary-type writing is in vogue almost everywhere creative writing is taught. So successful is this means for getting kids to write, that history, health, and psychology classes use it too!

This is a typical assignment: "Write something in your journal every day. It can be about your best friend, about your problems, about your parents—your innermost thoughts. Address it to 'yourself' or 'the author of the book you're reading.' You won't have to share it with anyone but me (the teacher)."

This is a borderline assignment—I've seen it on my English sub days. But it easily could leap the gap between writing techniques and "critical appraisals" of family members and "revealing mental and psychological problems." In fact, it needs no "interpretation" to see that this assignment violates the Hatch Amendment if used for any other purpose than to facilitate writing or research technique—and even then it is open to question because of the "unproven teaching methods" clause. (The Hatch Amendment says schools violate the law only when the assignment is solely for the purpose of psychological testing and behavior modification or for purposes of "developing new or unproven teaching methods or techniques.")

The Hatch Amendment also says it's up to the teacher to procure *parental permission before the fact.* My husband and I found many violations of this Pupil Protection Act when we dug through twenty-three years of our kids' school work. But by the time we knew our rights, it was too late.

One of our readers tells of her 1972 junior high viewing of Shirley Jackson's short story, "The Lottery." Widely promoted as good literature, it's a morbid play about random, lottery-style stoning. A mother is viciously stoned while her small son looks on. After showing the film, the junior high teacher delivered her deadly slips of paper. One child—our reader—picked the "blue" slip. Then the bell rang. No one told her what to do with her "lottery" ticket. This former student still carries the imprint of that horror. I don't know any parent who would sign approval for such an exercise!

Phyllis Schlafly's *Child Abuse in the Classroom*[7] is twenty-eight pages of editorial comment, three pages of legal rights, and 406 pages of unabridged parent testimony from Congressional hearings in Seattle, Pittsburgh, Kansas City, Phoenix, Concord, Orlando, and Washington, D.C. detailing examples like the one above. Some are milder. Some far worse.

What do these forty-five books have to do with this act? With the high rate of death, sexual permissiveness, and moronic fathers in these books, any assignment using such fiction could easily pass over the psychological "experimental" line. In fact, this kind of assignment could—and does—happen with the classics as well. *Siddhartha,*[8] a modern "classic," is taught complete with five lessons on transcendental meditation in at least one Iowa high school. This could explain why one Christian teacher was surprised to see her friend's son write a paper on the glories of transcendental meditation. I believe these religious experiments occur because parents don't take their responsibilities seriously. Parents who give up their rights should not holler "thief."

But is it enough to know your classroom rights? What about school district and state rights?

School Boards Are the Key

Even though some teacher groups want to *invert* the traditional pyramid, legally parents and community cap a power pyramid which flows *from* private citizens to school boards to administrators to teachers.[9] This power pyramid says teachers are my employees. School board members in my district are answerable to me. And to you.

Though each district writes the finer rules of time and place, every citizen has a right to be heard before the school board, which in most states must publish meeting dates and location. At my first Iowa school board meeting, I was the only one who sat through the whole meeting.

"Even though some teacher groups want to invert *the traditional pyramid, legally parents and community cap a power pyramid which* flows from *private citizens to school boards to administrators to teachers."*

The board was pleased and surprised to see me. "We don't get many people at the meetings," said one of my board friends. "They just come when there's controversy." Others I've talked to tell the same story: unless there's scheduled controversy, no one shows up.

School board members are the listening ear of the school district. Each member should be accessible to you. One of my board friends gets lots of calls—he's committed to the job description of open, friendly listening.

However, you may be in a community which dumped responsibility where it doesn't belong: Understandably, the board and administration now think they own the schools. Anything besides your "Good job—keep it up" will sound like "Get your hands up!" and it may be five school board meetings, fifty parent allies, and a hundred phone calls before you begin to break the power grid.

If you plan a curriculum challenge, know that you'll face a fortress—most of what's written in modern textbooks and library fiction is firmly planted on Dewey bedrock, where most teachers, administrators, and board members have either firm footing or firm pressure to stand pat. Traditional morality, creation science, and historically accurate patriotism may not fit the prescription of local entrenchment.

Citizen Input in State Curriculum Selection

Some states (like Maryland, California, and Texas) allow citizen input before textbook purchase. Publicly-announced sites display proposed texts for your comment. This includes the literature-based junior-high readers.

Some *local* school districts allow parental selection help. But dig deeper: you may find that this "call for parent help" is for tiny segments of curriculum, and that the "parent committee" is handpicked from a narrow philosophical segment of the district.

Your state School Boards Association (at the state capital) can tell you whether your state allows such input.

Please know that if your textbook challenge is about morality, historical accuracy, or patriotism, your words of wisdom will be considered "ideological attacks," and you are likely to be dismissed as "a tiny segment of the population."

State Records Are Your Records

Few people know they can ask for any public record. Except for individual citizen privacy or national security, state codes allow public scrutiny of everything from sewage-line bids to teacher salaries. You may have to pay for computer searches, but state records—no matter how embarrassing to public officials—are yours by right. Your library doesn't have the State code? You can get it from your state's legal office—ask for that portion which talks about public scrutiny and public-document access. This should be one of the first papers in your "do-something file."

You can ask for your child's file.

Your child's school file is yours for the asking. Most teachers and administrators are eager to assist. Did you find an error in your child's file? Ask to have it deleted. Check back in two months—see if it's gone. Check again in a year. This way, the error won't follow your child through thirteen years of school.

The Rights' Twin Sister: Responsibility

I have the *right* to read my child's textbook and school library fiction, but I may not recognize its twin sister: *responsibility*.

Have You Read a Good Textbook Lately?

It's intimidating to ask for your child's textbook—but you may have to if your teenager is one of those who "never gets homework." Sure— thirty parents checking out textbooks from a single classroom would greatly deplete the supply. But why not ask the school board to put one or two extras in the classroom just for Mom and Dad? Korean children get two textbooks—one for kids and one for parents.[10] When you've been to enough school board meetings, ask for town library shelf space for a copy of every textbook in the school system. If there are "not enough funds," suggest community "adopt-a-book" donations.

Maybe you can't take home fiction and texts. You may have to squirm and bear it—in a corner reading desk after school. I recommend this quiet time even if you *can* take the textbook home. Bulletin boards, the teacher's paperback "mini library" (most of which he bought him- self), and the current reading-project library cart make good browsing.

Ask your school office (when they're not busy) to copy a few pages of textbook or fiction—as long as you don't break copyright laws by doing more than a whole chapter or by copying 10 percent of the entire book. Offer to pay for it.

A good companion book for your textbook and fiction sleuthing is Paul Vitz's alarming and documented *Evidence of Bias in Our Children's Textbooks.*

Now that your textbook comprehension is well-muscled, you might try asking for those little curriculum supplements in the teacher's file drawers. They're yours to read—or copy. If you plan such a reading marathon, please don't mistake your teacher's hesitation for hostility. Reading parents haven't been leaping through his window by the doz- ens. He will be in shock. Besides, his frazzled schedule makes it almost impossible to add one more thing to the day. Just write a polite request accommodating yourself to his schedule. Twice, if you have to.

You may find, as did two parent friends of mine, a supplement which guides teenagers in numerology—and describes teens with certain numbers as "those who are interested in the occult." (Numerology is based on the belief that your name has complementary numbers which reveal your personality type.)

I've seen dozens of such Twilight Zone exercises recommended in teacher workshops and handbooks. Teachers are more than tempted to try them, because they're designed to strike a spark in unmotivated students.

Visit the Classroom

Check with your school board: what's the classroom visitation policy? Some schools let you pop in any time, but some refuse such visits. Claiming "sensitive classroom discussion" or "distraction to the class," some teachers hoard their privacy. Also complicating your decision to visit class is your teenager's threat to leave home if you show up. Visiting his class during a different period works best for the teenager, but a stalling teacher takes continued patience and persistence. Try "taking a course"—sign up for the whole nine weeks—go every day to get the flavor. And the whole story. If the teacher doesn't want you as her new student—keep asking. It's your right.

In January, 1991, I "enrolled" in a sixth grade sex education class and was courteously received by both principal and teacher. At unit's end, my young "desk mate" presented me with a special drawing and a thank-you for helping her with the crossword puzzle. That teacher's reputation was on the line because he knew my report would make the rounds as "representative" of the other sixth-grade teachers in our district. Also, my reputation as a fair reporter would reflect on two articulate and hard-working parents who'd spent hundreds of hours carefully researching current sex education materials.

You will find many teachers so thrilled with the prospect of a real live parent that they fall all over themselves to keep you in class. I don't know many teachers that would respond negatively to a well-stated visit which is thoroughly checked with principal and teacher. It is only if you are made to wait a week or given some vague reason for refusal that you should claim your rights. Imagine the confusion if every parent demanded a visit the first month of school! Cliff Schimmels' *How to Help Your Child Survive and Thrive in Public School*[11] puts the emphasis where it's needed—on good PR and support of your teacher: on understanding—not threats.

Focus on the Family documents a hidden sex education agenda via Planned Parenthood, in which visiting PP "instructors" glorify and promote teen sex. They hand out colored condoms, toning down jargon when a known parent is in the room.[12] Yours may be a school district where this subterfuge happens with alarming frequency. You may also be in a district where it *never* happens! Please do not assume that it is happening until you can prove it. "Innocent until proven guilty" is also a part of our Constitution!

Learn to pick up on your children's after-school moods: Try to be

---

> **"Try 'taking a course'—sign up for the whole nine weeks—go every day to get the flavor. And the whole story. If the teacher doesn't want you as her new student—keep asking. It's your right."**

---

there when they come home. The best way to spend the five minutes before you greet your after-school child is in prayer for wisdom.

Keep Current. Read. Listen. Ask.

It's fun to read about rights. It fills us with a sense of power—and anger, its frequent ally. Unfortunately, many parents operate on short-term fuses, demanding rights without responsibilities. What would happen if you *demanded* your responsibilities!?

I slogged through public school, college, and post-graduate work without one course in marriage or parenting. I learned those two subjects on the job. So it was news to me that one of my parenting assignments was to keep my public schools accountable. I believed the current wisdom: "You'll have seven daily hours of free time once your kids are in school."

I wasn't ready to copy the Japanese housewife who spends three after-school hours with her kids' homework each day. Or three hours while they're *in* school, reading their textbooks! But the other extreme is just as bad: reading half of one book is not research. Attending two PTA's a year is not fact-finding. Listening to a neighbor describe two pages of your child's textbook is not scientific inquiry. Faithfully subscribing to a fistful of conservative newsletters won't do the job!

Ironically, we Christians make the same mistake with which we credit our supposedly "liberal" counterparts—we don't think critically. We stuff ourselves with conservative views and think we have the whole truth. Subscribing to mainline periodicals isn't enough either. We need to dig deeper. We need to research for ourselves rather than filter the facts through our favorite national mentor.

In some circles I would be shot at dawn for suggesting this: I advise you to jog to the library once a month and read *The Humanist* cover to cover. Then you'll know who and what you're up against: an amazing array of public figures who prescribe an agenda with no moral absolutes. A generous American Humanist Association donor added another 2,000 gift subscriptions to the 5,324 *Humanist* subscriptions now populating our libraries.[13] Now your child reads *The Humanist* in her school library: shouldn't you grapple with it too?

While you're studying *The Humanist,* check the balance of tax-funded magazines in the school or town library. Do any of these periodicals champion the conservative cause? Do any of them tell you that Concerned Women for America has *three times* the membership of the National Organization of Women? (Have you ever seen CWA quoted in a major news source?) Did you find, as I did in a junior-high library, three magazines originating from the Soviet Embassy and not one on religious or conservative views? You'll likely find the same lack of diversity in your university libraries. Sure, you'll get more books in sheer numbers—but you're looking for new types of fruit, not more varieties of bananas.

Ask Questions from a Trusted Legal Source

I recommend *The Christian Legal Advisor* by John Eidsmoe—who comes complete with law degree and Master of Divinity.[14] His reference is a large, detailed discussion of everything from Constitutional historical precedents to finding a good lawyer. And so you'll know what kind of law may be practiced *against* you, I recommend George T. Grant's *Trial and Error: Understanding the American Civil Liberties Union* (Brentwood, TN: Wolgemuth & Hyatt, 1987).

Develop the Habit of Asking

But don't wait until you've read all the books to start. And remember: even informed people—*especially* informed people—ask questions. They don't count on their own opinions. "Experts" soon topple from their pedestals if they do nothing but spew wisdom to awestruck crowds.

Sit Alone With God. Asking is a lifelong skill. And it's best learned at the feet of the Savior, who gives wisdom in abundance. On those days when I take the time to sit with God first, instead of plowing ahead on my own strength, I have more than enough efficiency and peace. When I claim a snarled schedule that doesn't give me time alone with God, nothing seems to go right.

"True inspiration is anchored in diligent homework—an inspirer tightens his 'belt of truth' so his slacks aren't wrapped around his ankles."

Inspire Other Parents. Want to inspire people? Ask them questions! True inspiration comes from people who don't fall in love with their own words. True inspiration comes from people who *do* the words. If you're excited about your long-term strategy, you'll motivate others to stick with the battle.

Don't Confuse "Inspiring" with "Conspiring." People who *inspire* aren't concerned with personal success. They're always looking for ways they can praise others for jobs well done. By contrast, a *conspiratorial* tone gets immediate attention, but can't hold the battle. That's because the conspiratorial tone is self-centered and pride-motivated.

With hushed, urgent tones, the "conspirer" says, "I hear the superintendent wants sex clinics—we gotta do something."

The "inspirer" says, "Walt, you've been keeping up with school issues. Do you know anything about the school board's attitude towards sex clinics? Would you go to the board meeting with me tonight and find out?"

True inspiration is anchored in diligent homework—an inspirer tightens his "belt of truth" so his slacks aren't wrapped around his ankles. Inspirers trust the other guy's ability to grow and get the job done. Inspiration takes attention off *self*.

The new "self-esteem" movement collapses under its own weight of self-centeredness. But rewrapped in fresh labels, the movement sprouts new gurus every year. It doesn't take much logic to see that self-esteem—for kids or adults—doesn't come from pumping up the ego. It comes from helping others. Having God's esteem is even better: It isn't the frustrating dead-end of making yourself look better. God does it for you if you're willing to use His label.

Strategy: 10 weeks—10 months—10 years

Armed now with facts, friendship, and prayer, all we need is cooperation to put the puzzle together.

Long-Term Action

Until we're well-read and sure of our rights, let's concentrate on building our base. If parental involvement has been eroding for sixty years, obviously our first effort should be to build a base of cooperation. Did someone call you to bake cookies? Bake plenty! Is there a football game? Go! PTA? Attend! If your child doesn't perform well in your district's public school, take her out. But if you want her there—or can't afford to take her out—*treat the school like the family it is*: write notes of encouragement. Make suggestions. Show up! One of our local principals, Jim Jackson, is a walking encouragement machine. To every child in his path there is a pat, a hug, or a compliment. But where does he get *his* fuel? Does he get it from you the parent?

One of our friends documents a three-year waiting period in a sluggish PTA. At just the right moment of his third year, he suggested parent involvement in an area previously sacred to administration. He was heard with respect for three reasons:

He'd put in his time.

He was willing to volunteer for the new job.

He didn't act like he knew it all.

Now this group is mushrooming—and cooperating with parent leadership to fight drugs and teen sexual activity!

Three years ago five of our readers got our feet wet in a pilot "self-esteem" program for one of our elementary schools. Our project leader recognized early that a chapter *appendix* system was the way to write

---

"Having an education philosophy isn't just for the teaching professional. Parents need one too! Instead of waiting for the next disastrous set of National Education Association goals, we can outflank with our own drumbeat."

---

balance into the project. Working with a cooperative school counselor, we added our ideas to counter person-centered philosophy. After working months on two hundred curriculum pages, our efforts were applauded by the program's in-class parent volunteers. They gobbled up our suggestions and asked for more.

Long-Term Goal

I'll never forget my first teaching interview. I had all my answers ready but one. Fifteen minutes into the conference, the graying, slim superintendent leaned over the desk, fixed me with his one brown and one blue eye and said, "And now, Miss Clarkson. What is your philosophy of education?" I don't remember what I said. But I know how I *sounded!* Just like a candidate for Miss America: bland, off-the-cuff, and boring. I learned my lesson before the second interview, and got the next job I tried for.

Having an education philosophy isn't just for the teaching professional. Parents need one too! Instead of waiting for the next disastrous set of National Education Association goals, we can outflank with our own drumbeat.

Our third and youngest child graduated from high school in 1989. But our family still has three long-term educational goals:

1. To research and document the public school agenda.
2. To be available for encouragement and information.
3. To pass to our grandchildren a love of Truth.

Being concerned with nothing but our own children's education is utterly selfish—and foolish. As an active citizen I buy from shopkeepers who are home-fed on public education values. I get well or die under the hands of doctors who grew up in America's schools. I drive cars bolted together by mechanics and assembly-line workers who learn the Dewey creed. I want these people to learn something better than selfish relativism. I want to learn something better for *myself*—the most stubborn student of all.

Group Power and Discernment

Any strategy lasting longer than several weeks gets boring, depressing, and lonely. That's why any long-range strategy needs group power. It needs prayer. Without these two dynamics we're accountable to no one but our own faulty reasoning. Without these dynamics "discernment" can't grow. Without these dynamics we lose the big picture and start believing the old tired jargon.

One such "dynamic" is Moms in Touch—made up of hundreds of small groups of five to ten mothers praying for local schools and children. Such power knifes through old resentments and unforgiveness—nationally, thousands of mothers give testimony to changed lives, re-invigorated parent-teacher relationships, and a new way of looking at their children's curriculum. When it's time to act, they know it! They're beginning to discern.

The second month of our local Moms in Touch, six good friends gathered around me and prayed: They prayed about my resentments against two teachers. They prayed for me to give up my need to orchestrate our son's senior year. They prayed that I would unpack my burden.

I did. Release is taught by the Master: there are no short courses. He taught me to speak a new language.

Discerning Jargon and "Doublespeak." If you want to win a war, first change the language. Nowhere was this more true than when American soldiers occupied Japan in post-War 1945. One dark night, frustrated Japanese citizens removed all English street signs and replaced them with original Japanese script, hurling American soldiers into bedlam at dawn. Those soldiers were stuck. They couldn't move further than one block without getting lost. Their signposts were gone and there was no sense in even *trying* to move until they'd carefully made new labels.

Vietnam days saw an American public furious with "euphemistic" descriptions of mass slaughter—from "anti-personnel" bombs to "friendly fire." The Persian Gulf conflict saw a change from "body bags" to "human remains pouches."

Abortion battle slogans change whenever political choreographers sense new direction in the political breeze. When "pro-abortion" doesn't work, it becomes "pro-choice." When "pro-life" begins to sway would-be-mothers, "anti-abortion" or "anti-choice" takes its place.

If "homosexual" is blighted, along comes "gay" to brighten the dreary scenery.

Under these new rules, women can be "feminists." Men can be . . . well—could they get by with being "masculinists"?

When "values-clarification" education revealed its true colors—as a method of changing children's values—educators scrambled to spruce up the lingo: now we have "values understanding" or "self-esteem." A very bright parent can feel very stupid when blitzed with changing educational lexicons. Here are some of those "educational" definitions:

- Censor: Anyone who challenges book content.

- Variable censor: School librarian who censors out such obviously pornographic literature as *Playboy*.

- Pre-emptive censor: Librarian, publisher, or reviewer who makes literary and quantifiable judgments for book or library content.

- Editor: One who decides which parts of the book or paper are worth publishing. He/she can also "censor" profanities from direct quotes.

- Values clarification: System of educating a child to change his values by making him see that his values and those of his parents and church are outdated.

- Values understanding: Same as above. New jargon to replace the failed phrase. Used in particular by Planned Parenthood.

- Critical thinking: Method of allowing a child her own moral decisions based on having all the facts. Many "traditional" or Judeo-Christian facts are missing. (In this system, there is no right or wrong.)

- Outercourse: Replaces "intercourse" in some sex education curricula. Refers to *any* sexual activity except anal or vaginal intercourse. Suggested as a logical alternative to intercourse.

- Situation ethics: Nothing is right or wrong. Everything is relative to the situation. It's right if you think it's right; wrong if you think it's wrong.

- Multi-cultural, non-sexist education: Leans heavily towards global, one-world concepts. Blurs gender identity and traditional male/female roles.

- Survival: Classroom game—students must decide who will live or die based on worth.

- Magic circle or peer circle: Students sit in a circle and discuss their feelings with the teacher as psycho-therapeutic facilitator.

- Self-esteem: Catch-all for programs designed to make the student feel good about herself so she won't do drugs or fail academically. Focuses on self.

- Consciousness or inner self: Can be an avenue towards understanding "self" or "getting in touch with self." This is a readiness technique for meditation.

- Relaxation: A technique which sometimes leads to meditation.

- Academic Freedom: Teachers have freedom to teach. Kids have freedom to learn. Parents have no say.

New Age. Missing from this list is the entire new age lexicon. "New age" is a catch-all for everything that smacks of Eastern philosophies or occult thinking. Two types of people muddy the waters here—those who don't see the danger in anything new age, and those who see crystals and Zen Buddhas under every textbook. A good start to unraveling this philosophical yarn is *Understanding the New Age*, by Los Angeles Times religion writer Russell Chandler.[15]

For help with the wider education picture I recommend *Parents' Rights* by John W. Whitehead.[16] Though he doesn't list "rights" in super-market order, you'll catch the concept of the "adultified child" philosophy—emerging childrens' "rights" that ram family structure head on.

Now—Act!

For the action-oriented, this is the fun part—until we realize that it might take six months of preparation for six minutes of action!

"To be effective, you'll need every ounce of preparation we've described so far. If you don't prepare, you'll hear yourself backfire in the next county."

If you're an old hand, you'll know that "action" is part of everything we've been talking about so far—it's prayer, research, running for office, encouragement, respect, baking cookies, asking questions, committing to meetings, and showing up.

But there are those exciting—sometimes horrifying—moments that most people consider parent "action." It's what most people would like to *start* with.

I'm talking about the letters to the editor, the speeches at school board meetings, and your trip to the school library. To be effective, you'll need every ounce of preparation we've described so far. If you don't prepare, you'll hear yourself backfire in the next county.

Parents in the Cleveland, Oklahoma, school district did their homework before they confronted the school board about occult books. Parents specifically objected to two books in their middle school library with "how-to" satanic hexes but no warning of its dangers. In a calm, well-documented letter to the school board, the spokesparent wrote that both books "prompt the reader to investigate activities that are not appropriate to social be-havior," and treat Christianity in an "inaccurate light."[17]

Using the school board's own Library Bill of Rights, they proved the school system didn't follow its own mandate to "provide materials which accurately reflect all religious, social, political and ethnic groups, and their contributions to our American heritage as well as a knowledge and appreciation of world history and culture."[18]

People for the American Way lists this parent "action" as a censor-ship attempt. PFAW says parents "erroneously" argued such books far outweigh any other religion in the library.[19] But Cleveland parents say that wasn't their statement: Their claim was that occult books far out-weigh "books of like kind."

The Cleveland school superintendent was caught—in the middle of a profession which abhors censorship, and an awareness that community occult activity was a growing threat. But neither group was helped by PFAW's account of the "censorship attempt." They both say it is not totally accurate.[20]

These Oklahoma parents' "action" isn't finished. Their follow-through includes making sure the school board reads all the occult books which it promised to examine after taking them from the middle school—and putting them in the high school library.

How to Make a Book Challenge

It's good corporate philosophy: take grievances to your immediate superior. The same is true with book challenges. However, before you call the prin-cipal or ask the librarian for a book-challenge form, do your homework:

1. Ask the school board (because you want them to take notice and be accountable) for curriculum-selection guidelines. Study them with a trusted friend.

2. Ask the school district's head librarian for library-selection guidelines. Study them.

3. When you know which parts of the guide may have been vio-lated, read your books again to see where the problem lies. Some books in high school libraries easily fall under the anti-obscenity laws. (We may well have one in our list of forty-five.) Don't be afraid to challenge according to these statutes.

4. If you want more diversity in your library's fiction, start by asking for the current fiscal-year "library purchasing order" (some purchase orders mix the fiction with the non-fiction). Randomly select—by computer or alphabetically picking a sequential number, until you have at least a tenth of the books—a third is better. If the list is too long, randomly select from the latest publishing year.

   Read them. You may want to purchase them directly or check them out from the town library—if you ask for them at the school library, you might as well tape a sign on your back. You can use our book form. Or you can use your own. A word of caution here: This method is hard, painstaking work—it should be done well or not at all.

5. Find a small group of parents who has time to study the books. Keep your project confidential—not because of any clandestine motives—but because any premature comment will return to you with ripe embellishments. In 1987 I mistakenly made a challenge—without long-term homework—at an open meeting. I hardly recognized "my" comments as they later came home to roost with sticky chicken feet.

6. When you've read the books and matched them to school system guidelines, ask the school board the average length of time it takes to act on a "book challenge form." Fill out this library "form" and enclose a cover letter stating your concerns. Send a copy to the librarian, the principal, the superintendent, and the school board. Wait a week.

7. If needed, send another letter. Wait another week. Call the school principal. Arrange for a meeting if you are stalled. If you are not satisfied:

8. Ask for response time on the school board docket. You've been attending board meetings regularly, so this should be no problem.

9. Don't confuse stalling with foul play. Always assume the best from your school district. Their time pressures are enormous, just as yours are. Treat them with respect through every stage of your dealings. Calling in press or attorney *should not* be your first action!

10. *Document everything: Phone calls, letters, conversations. Keep your word. Be above-board. Pray.*

11. Suggest *or donate* books to fill out your library's balance. Your school should have a donation plan. If not, you can walk in the footsteps of Dorothy Bearss of Oxnard, California and talk to your administration—first about the lack of diversity, then about your community's willingness to donate.[21] In 1990 I was so impressed with a new conservative magazine's in-depth reporting, that I donated *New Dimensions* to our public library.[22] I did so after thoroughly researching the diversity of the library's other news magazines. I was extremely well received, and the library is grateful for the gift. And yes, it's on the shelf.

Initiate Change

Now you know because you're part of the plan: the difference between parents who react—and parents who initiate and plan—is the difference between success and failure.

- Initiators see the wider picture. Responders and reactors run in narrow circles.

- Initiators are willing to change their image from second-class responders.

- Initiators keep ten-year goals and commitments.

- Initiators have vision and wisdom to shape more than just current events: They have a centennial, God-centered philosophy of education.

For parents willing to put all their trust in God and to put their family on the line, I promise you more than enough work. I promise you misunderstandings, short-term failures, and fatigue.

But I promise you success where it counts—in "obeying God rather than men," for your family, and for public school kids who deserve more diversity than they're getting.

"Treat [your school district] with respect through every stage of your dealings."

7

From California To Ohio: What's in The Libraries and How Parents Helped Change Them

W orking with your public library to insure diversity is *not* censorship! Logic says it. Parents say it. The dictionary says it. And yes, People for the American Way says it. In answer to my first letter detailing racial and job-role imbalance in teen fiction, People for the American Way said:

"We applaud your commitment to redressing the imbalances you describe in your school's library. . . . a reasonable request to the library staff will let them know what kinds of materials you'd like to see more of, and most librarians are only to [sic] happy to respond to parental enthusiasm about good books." They went on to suggest parental involvement in library selection, library sale of "older or more outdated" books to provide money for new books, and donation of books "in specific areas."[1]

People for the American Way never answered my second letter, in which I specifically asked for help in creating diversity in libraries which overstock books omitting or profaning the Christian lifestyle.

I also got helpful hints from a *Better Homes and Gardens* article which said to "Dial 1–800 for Education."[2] Here's what they sent me: a tool kit for reducing male and female "stereotyping" in curriculum, all written by the National Committee for Citizens in Education and produced by the U. S. Department of Education. There isn't enough, it seems, of mothers who work and fathers who do domestic chores in today's curricula.

But enough of funded groups and government help. What I really wanted was proof of parent action. What's in real libraries across the country? What do everyday, normal American parents do about their tax-supported libraries?

What Happened in Hiawatha, Kansas?

Staci Charles of Hiawatha, Kansas thought she was a normal parent. Raising her own and helping with three others in her small day care, this former teacher has loved books since she was a kid. So it was a natural move to update her teaching certificate with a course on "young adult" literature in 1988.

In a Tele-Net lecture for 160 Kansas librarians, Charles learned she was not a normal parent but a crazy one. At least that's what the librarians in the lecture room called any parent who challenged book content.

After reading seventeen of the five hundred ALA-recommended books on the class list, she despaired of finding one understanding parent, one sensible Christian—one positive use of God's name. After more research (Vitz's curriculum study and phone calls to Christian publishers—and more fiction reading. Lots more), Charles shared her findings with the class:

"We've been talking a lot about censorship," said Staci Charles over the Tele-Net microphone. "But I've read numerous books on the ALA Best Books list. I know there are many books offered by Christian publishers which are conspicuously missing from this list. So the only evidence of censorship I see is on the part of the Library Association and other national book lists which ignore fiction with any Christian or conservative views." Silence. Glares.

An angry librarian broke the silence. "If you feel that way, don't ever become a librarian; librarians have to be liberals."

The entire class then bombarded her with the usual questions: "What is it you don't like—the profanity? The sex?"

Charles answered: "It isn't so much what's *on* the list that I don't like but what is *missing* from the list." She told them about well-written, best-selling Christian books with millions of copies to their credit.

"Where are these books?" they scoffed.

"Precisely my point," said Charles. "You don't see these books because reviewers won't review them and best-books lists don't include them. This censorship is worse than the small number of complaints you get from parents."

"I know there are many books offered by Christian pubishers which are conspicuously missing from this list. So the only evidence of censorship I see is on the part of the Library Association and other national book lists which ignore fiction with any Christian or conservative views."

None of them believed Christian books were any good. Charles set out to prove otherwise. A "prompting from God" led her to a sympathetic Christian bookstore owner who loaned her all the books she needed to hand out samples at the next class.

Suddenly Poison

With the instructor's permission she passed her books around. No one would touch them or talk to her. Her ideas and her books were poison. "Labeled and segregated I was shamed to silence the remainder of the class period. Weren't these very people calling for pluralism and new ideas a week ago?" wondered Charles.

Furious and shaken, Charles realized she needed Christ's calming love to speak through her. Finally, with one well-chosen positive statement each week, she saw the class begin to soften. More and more classmates borrowed books and thanked Charles for bringing them. When her instructor asked for printed lists of "good Christian books" to distribute to the class, Charles was elated.

"How I love to boast of God's power!" she says.

With this major victory behind her Staci Charles tried the same rhetoric of balance and gift books with her public and middle-school libraries. She donated:

- *This Present Darkness.* Frank Peretti. (Crossway, Westchester, IL, 1986).

- *The Gates of Zion.* Bodie Thoene. (Bethany House, Minneapolis, 1986).

- *Dream Thief.* Steven Lawhead. (Crossway, Westchester, IL, 1983).

- *Code of Honor.* Sandy Dengler. (Bethany House, Minneapolis, 1988).

- *Colorado Gold.* Marian Wells. (Bethany House, Minneapolis, 1988).

By spring the public librarian had stocked sequel books to Peretti's, Thoene's, and Dengler's books at reader request.

By fall 1990, her middle school librarian had begun stocking Christian books, and the high school was well on its way with another helpful Charles donation: *The Christian Book Distributor's* magazine.

But she and several friends still wondered: *What was in the teen fiction or "young adult" literature section of their public library? Had it begun to show better results than our list of forty-five from 1988?* No one wanted to *ban* books. But was there room to suggest diversity? Though the town librarian left most of the "top-recommended" books to the high-school librarian to stock, her own books were from those same review lists—*Booklist* and *Library Journal.*

Results of the Questionnaire

Using my questionnaire, the Hiawatha group checked out eighteen of the new fiction offerings at the town library—almost all of the new (mostly 1990) books. Their random method was simply to check out every book that was still on the shelf. (Few "adult books recommended for young adults" are on teen library shelves; however, they're in the adult section.

This leaves the "young adult" shelves with somewhat lower profanity and sexual activity than you might find in a public school library.)

Here's what they found:

Lagging Dads. In fiction two years newer than our Project 45, fathers and husbands are *still* portrayed more negatively than moms and wives. There were even more female authors in the Hiawatha group— more female protagonists—than in our forty-five.

Top Teens. Teens were king (nope—queen) of the hill, and they asked others for help twice as often as they asked their parents. If you were under six or over fifty-five, you didn't have much chance for stardom in these books.

Profanity. Profanity? About the same as the forty-five—slightly lower in the "frequent" to "continual" range. Two-thirds of the books had it.

Personal God. "Personal God" themes didn't get the scathing negatives of our forty-five. But still they dragged their feet behind other world-life views. Capping only 20 percent of the total, none of the books followed the "personal God" theme throughout (and only one "frequent use" tally). God was present for roll call, but did kids rely on Him to solve their problems? No—or at least for only 4 percent of their problems.

"I Loved It!" or "It Was Junk!" Reader response was half negative, half positive. Off-the-cuff comments ranged from "horrible" and "junk" to "really good" and "I loved this book." No one wanted to purchase a book, even though these parents read plenty and encourage their kids to do the same.

Safe Sex? Only a third of the books left this subject alone, with slightly more authors showing approval for teen sex than not.

White, White, White. The 80 percent whites didn't leave much room for other races. But though Native Americans cornered only 2 percent of the total, they were 100 percent positive. Blacks didn't fare much better in numbers—only 5 percent of total—but they were also 100 percent positive! And most of the books we read in all four projects showed white suburban or small-town kids at least two-to-one in favor of city, inter-racial, or multi-cultural.

Without Benefit of Clergy. Hiawatha readers found only one positively portrayed clergy out of 38 authority figures and 141 main characters. We wondered what happened to that profession. Teachers didn't do so well, either—only half were in positive roles. In fact, in almost every category, authority figures were more wishy-washy than they were positive.

Handicaps. One Alzheimer's patient completed this picture. There were none of the "incidental" characters we'd hoped for.

The Library Responds

Because Staci Charles had laid a solid-gold pathway of respect, research and patience, the town librarian now knew her as helpful—not a threat. But two years before, the librarian had wondered: Why would a "normal" parent like Staci want the inter-library loan of an inflammatory title like *Book Burning*?

After two years of encouragement and book gifts, even Charles' four-page teen-book analysis was no longer a threat. In fact, Charles could say with complete honesty that the library seemed to be more diverse than it was two years before. The big compliment to that librarian was that she did an excellent job with the lists she had to work with!

Parent Plan: Part Two

Now it was time for part 2 of the Charles Encouragement Plan. In part 1, Charles had donated adult novels with Christian themes. Now, she left the librarian with a gift check and *The Christian Book Distributor* and asked *the librarian* to pick the teen fiction books!

I join her in boasting of God's power!

Hiawatha Public Library
1990 Teen Fiction Books Reviewed by Parents

- Adler, Carol S. *The Lump in the Middle*. Clarion Books, 1989.
- Baehr, Patricia. *Falling Scales*. Morrow Junior Books, 1987.

"Hiawatha readers found only one positively portrayed clergy out of 38 authority figures and 141 main characters."

- Carter, Alden R. *Sheilah's Dying.* G. P. Putnam's Sons, 1987.

- Crutcher, Chris. *Chinese Handcuffs.* Greenwillow Books, 1989.

- Duncan, Lois. *Don't Look Behind You.* Delacorte Press. Bantam/Doubleday/Dell, 1989.

- Kingsolver, Barbara. *The Bean Trees.* Harper and Row, 1988.

- Klein, Norma. *Going Backwards.* Scholastic, 1986.

- Landis, James D. *Looks Aren't Everything.* Bantam, 1990.

- Myers, Walter Dean. *Scorpions.* Harper and Row, 1988.

- Myers, Walter Dean. *Fallen Angels.* Scholastic, 1988.

- Naylor, Phyllis Reynolds. *The Year of the Gopher.* Atheneum, 1987.

- Nelson, Theresa. *And One for All.* Orchard Books, 1989.

- Nixon, Joan Lowery. *The Other Side of Dark.* Delacorte, 1986.

- Peck, Richard. *Princess Ashley.* Delacorte, 1987.

- Pevsner, Stella. *How Could You Do It, Diane?* Clarion, 1989.

- Sleator, William. *The Boy Who Reversed Himself.* E. P. Dutton, 1986.

- Sleator, William. *Strange Attractions.* E. P. Dutton, 1990.

- Voigt, Cynthia. *Seventeen Against the Dealer.* Atheneum, 1990.

Minneapolis: Suburban Teens

Near Minneapolis a low, brick building sprawls near a major thoroughfare. Inside are one thousand students who reflect the 5 percent minority and 50 percent blue-collar/white-collar mix of its community. Smiling, helpful secretaries and librarians shout the first message: kids are loved in this school. But the library list from this junior high tells us those one thousand kids are reading the same thing that kids in New York, Idaho, and Mississippi get. Randomly, we read from their 1989 and 1990 purchase lists:

- Bridgers, Sue Ellen. *Permanent Connections*. Harper & Row, 1987.

- Brooks, Terry. *The Elfstones of Shannara*. Random House, 1977.

- Colman, H. *The Double Life of Angela Jones*. Morrow Junior Books, 1988.

- Conford, Ellen. *Strictly for Laughs*. Berkley/Pacer, 1987.

- Davis, Jenny. *Good-bye and Keep Cold*. Orchard Books, 1987.

- Dickinson, Peter. *The Devil's Children*. Laurel-Leaf, 1987.

- Irwin, Hadley. *Abby, My Love*. Atheneum, 1985.

- Kahn, J. *Return of the Jedi*. Ballantine, 1983.

- Lewis, C. S. *The Silver Chair*. Macmillan, 1980.

- Lively, P. *The Ghost of Thomas Kempe*. E. P. Dutton, 1973.

- Pierce, T. *In the Hand of the Goddess*. Atheneum, 1984.

- Salassi, O. R. *Jimmy D., Sidewinder, and Me*. Greenwillow, 1987.

- Springer, Nancy. *Not on a White Horse*. Alfred A. Knopf, 1988.

- Tolan, Stephanie S. *The Great Skinner Getaway*. Puffin, 1988.

- Willey, M. *If Not for You*. Harper & Row, 1988.

- Yolen, Jane. *Heart's Blood*. Dell, 1986.

Though we didn't make a *formal* study of these books, we found these trends: kids solve their own problems, and the traditional God of the Bible is either outdated or doesn't apply. It's an all-white collection, too, with almost the only exception a group of noble Sikh (combination Moslem-Hindu faith) warriors who rescue kidnapped British children from bigoted country folk. In fact, we saw this pseudo-Hindu philosophy repeated in five of the books. In the seven books which deal with non-marital sex, going to bed is tabu only when forced. Marriage is 60 percent negative.

Once again, immensely talented authors got us goose-bumpy, laughing, and sidetracked. But in nine books, Dad's either missing, misinformed, or abusive. Parents—if not dead—are slightly worse than neutral. The only good parents tend to be dominated by Mom. Clergy are bigoted, bumbling, or banished. A third of the books had spirit-centered overtones.

The one positive personal-God novel, *Silver Chair,* kept this junior high collection from soaring off the person-centered, fate, and impersonal-spirits theme charts. Thankfully, alcohol and tobacco use were low. But our five readers thought only five of these fifteen books were of sufficient quality for their kids to read alone.

We looked east of the Mississippi for our next round.

Columbus, Ohio: Inner City Teens

Briggs High School of inner-city Columbus, Ohio is 51 percent ethnic minorities (mostly Black) and 49 percent Caucasian. Parents in this court-desegregated school are mostly blue-collar. So I hoped library fiction characters would reflect the mix. Right? Not so. With a tight review list to choose from, even schools like Briggs could not find quality literature to speak to their ethnically-mixed clientele. I'd read twenty-one of those books already (randomly selected from other lists) and except for Walter Myers' strong black characters in *Fallen Angels,* and *Red Storm's* tiny cameos of a black officer and an Asian pilot, I hadn't met any ethnic minorities in those books. I hoped our *random* reading list would prove me wrong.

I was warned of other problems, too. Jim McCarty, English teacher and reading instructor at Briggs, said Biblically-based literature is diminishing year by year. He taught "The Bible as Literature" until 1980, but, as in other schools around the country, it hasn't been taught since. And in updated literature texts available to Briggs, McCarty said the Good Samaritan Story was replaced with "The Killing of John Dillinger."

It concerns Jim that he regularly sees students displaying occult signs on their hands, reading occult themes in their newer library fiction, and sneaking looks at dime-store occult comic books during class. Paired with this tendency is the ten-year trend towards newer library books which describe sex in more vivid, descriptive language and illustrations.

But there's good news for this school: Briggs boasts a lower teacher-student ratio than most high schools, and they have a successful work-study program. McCarty is relieved, too, that his library doesn't have adult novelists like Judith Krantz. Some high schools do.

McCarty says the disturbing new fiction themes don't affect most of the students. Only 10 to 15 percent of them get their literature from free-reading fiction. But the avid readers—our future leaders—gobble these themes. "The over-achiever is bored with regular assignments," he says. "You'll see these kids reading two or three new fiction books a day." McCarty agrees that it's the top-IQ kids—the next generation of leaders—who are absorbing these new-fiction ideas.

Briggs librarian Karen Wagstaff, a nineteen-year veteran media specialist, was "surprised and sad" at most of our findings. She had suspected that authors took pot shots at clergy, and fiction parents were less than noble. But when she saw actual statistics showing so few minority characters, she was extremely disappointed. She agreed there should be more—especially for a school with the Briggs ethnic mix.

The negative authority figures and teens who outflanked their elders disturbed her, too. These newer books were supposed to be the ones that "dealt with problems—like (Lois) Duncan's books—not the hunky-dory endings of a generation ago." And when she learned of the barren wasteland of personal-God-centered themes, she said: "I don't know how I can fit one more thing into my schedule. But in light of this—all I can say is that I will make every effort to look for a wider diversity of book reviews." Her "minimal budget" allows for two main fiction-review services: *School Library Journal* and *Booklist*. She had thought them quite adequate. Until now.

Here's what three of our readers found in these fifteen randomly-picked 1988–89-purchased novels:

- Adler, C. S. *Kiss the Clown*. Clarion Books, 1986.
- Asher, Sandy. *Everything is Not Enough*. Delacorte Press, 1987.
- Bess, Clayton. *Tracks*. Houghton-Mifflin, 1986.
- Conford, Ellen. *Seven Days to a Brand-New Me*. Little, Brown and Co., 1981.

- Crutcher, Chris. *Stotan!* Greenwillow, 1986.

- Duncan, Lois. *The Third Eye.* Little, Brown and Co., 1984.

- Ferris, Jean. *Invincible Summer.* Farrar/Straus/Giroux, 1987.

- Kerr, M. E. *Night Kites.* Harper and Row, 1986.

- Levoy, Myron. *Pictures of Adam.* Harper and Row, 1986.

- Malmgren, Dallin. *The Whole Nine Yards.* Laurel-Leaf/Delacorte, 1986.

- Marlin, J. *Appeal to the Heart.* Berkley/Pacer, 1987.

- Pfeffer, Susan Beth. *Getting Even.* Berkley/Pacer, 1987.

- Thompson, Julian. *A Band of Angels.* Scholastic, 1986.

- Voigt, Cynthia. *The Runner.* Ballantine/Fawcett Juniper, 1985.

- Zindel, Paul. *Pardon Me, You're Stepping on my Eyeball!* Harper and Row, 1976.

Fathers in Briggs literature were a notch or two higher than mothers. But marriage took a lethal shot in the heart. Parents who were most likely to give serious effort to marriage were killed off near the first chapter. In fact, authority figures of all stripes wallowed in a 60 percent negative pool. Clergy bowed to government, though, for the honor of receiving the least positives. (It's okay if you're a Democrat. In 500 recent young adult novels, I have yet to see Republicans—whether dog-catchers or presidents—mentioned with kindness.)

Teenagers in these senior high books were sharper—and more sexually active—than their middle-school or junior high counterparts (one

---

"'The over-achiever is bored with regular assignments,' he says. 'You'll see these kids reading two or three new fiction books a day.' McCarty agrees that it's the top-IQ kids—the next generation of leaders—who are absorbing these new-fiction ideas."

book condoned homosexuality). Forty-five percent of all characters were teens, and they were 63 percent positive, able to leap tall problems with a single bound—dazzling their often-befuddled parents. The middle-aged accounted for a third of the characters, but surprisingly, they were less negative than the nineteen through thirty-six-year-old young adults. There were four times as many babies as oldsters—but even taken together, this bunch of young and old comprised only 8 percent of the total.

Caucasians took 87 percent of all characters. Even more alarming: *All protagonists were white.* A biracial teenager in one book was beautifully characterized, but the novel (promoting non-marital sex and occult practices) has appalled more than one parent, who found it in another state's junior high book fare. Its book jacket glows with wholesome goodness.

No book had an inner-city setting, unless we count Seattle's *Stotan!* and Boston's *Getting Even,* which had some big city scenes. But *Stotan!* did give us secondary black characters, and an expanded role in the positive Asian-American coach (with a heady dose of Zen).

Homemakers got the axe. Only one of our twenty-two mothers was a positive homemaker (the other good homemaker was a grandmother). And the only positive blue collar workers were kids doing minimum wage. Again we get the message: either get your own business, or put on a white collar.

Fate themes brush-stroked a third of these books a dull gray. "Loving Personal God" themes took only 5 percent of all the positives—while person-centered took 60 percent! Maybe that's why our three readers were "resentful, depressed or disappointed" with half their books. But we'll take good news where we can get it: a fourth of the books left readers with some hopeful, laughing or "understanding" thoughts. Tobacco use followed the national trend of low popularity. The best news of all: this inner-city librarian and at least one of Briggs' teachers care enough to find other review sources with which to diversify their teen fiction.

Kansas City: Heartland of America

On her way down the hallway to the Plaza Middle School library, Stephanie Carlson watched the students carefully. Here were the characters she might sketch in a future book. Carlson, a dental assistant, hoped to write and illustrate her own children's books, and she was glad to be back in the "word" business again. A real mimic, she savored words like a chocolate addict delights in turtle pie.

> *"If it hadn't been for the Pakistani-Islamic personal-God theme in the award-winning* **Shabanu,** *there would be little in these books of a "positive" personal God. Fate, impersonal spirits, and a person-centered ethic dominated 83 percent of the books."*

Balancing an armful of middle school books, she parceled them out to her Bible Study fellowship group and kept some for herself. That first evening, she cracked open *Genie with the Light Blue Hair.* One page into the Groucho Marx genie who could say "Okey Dokey" before you could retract a wish, Carlson was committed to finish before morning. It could truthfully be said that she laughed herself to sleep.

But the next five books weren't so funny. Weird life-size wooden dolls, a dead girl in the fourth dimension—and what seemed surely to be real elves next door—disturbed what sleep is left to dental assistants who work double shifts.

The Ever-Shifting Compass

Were the other readers in her parent group reading the same types of stories? They were. Oh—it wasn't that the books weren't fun. They were. But they were disturbing, too. Profanity wasn't the problem. Sex wasn't the problem. They were rare in middle-school books. It was the child's need to work out his own problems from an ever-shifting compass of fourth dimensions and fatalism which disturbed them the most. When their own kids were old enough for middle school, these parents hoped there would be more personal God-centered books to balance the collection.

If it hadn't been for the Pakistani-Islamic personal-God theme in the award-winning *Shabanu*, there would be little in these books of a "positive" personal God. Fate, impersonal spirits, and a person-centered ethic dominated 83 percent of the books. And just as we found in Hiawatha, kids used God as a problem-solving tool only 4 percent of the time.

Once again, respect for clergy dropped off the cliff with the one negative portrayal—or half of one percent of total characters. In fact, there were only *thirteen* total authority figures out of 134 characters (almost half of whom were middle-school or teenage kids).

Kids, Do You Know Where Your Parents Are? This middle school—the youngest of all groups we studied—had access to fiction in which kids leaned on their parents only a fifth as often as they leaned on anyone else! Other kids, then other adults, beat out parents four to one.

Would You Purchase This Book? Finally! One book in 87 that someone wanted to purchase! *Shabanu* was the winner. It might be on some parent's shelf now, delighting its reader for the second time around. And the rest of the books? Parents said they would leave their kids alone to read them without parent input in only 12 percent of the cases!

Whiter than White. Once again, Causasians got the lion's share of the major characters. In fact, it could be said that *all* characters were somewhat Caucasian in their portrayal. This reading group saw no fictional blacks, Hispanics, or Orientals for their school in a mostly white, middle-class neighborhood.

Handicaps. The one handicap portrayal was a "blend" of good and bad. It was a scene that could frighten and hearten at the same time: a young girl pretends all is well in her darkly-shuttered house. Her father skipped town, so she steals, lies, and manipulates to get food for her desperately sick mother. No one knows of her need until book's end: it's an eleven-year-old girl and her sick mother against the world.

A Very Happy Librarian

All these books added up to a one-dimension view of life, and Stephanie Carlson's group had pages of objective data to prove it. But they weren't looking forward to telling the librarian. Unlike some crusading stumpers, this parent group preferred to bring *good* news, and not confront with negative documentation alone.

So they bought books. And Carlson made a list of other books so Plaza Middle School librarian Ted Derrick could select quickly. Others in her group cheered her on and prayed as she talked with the school.

Derrick was delighted—and surprised—with the group report and their offer of gift books. After nineteen years as a fifth grade teacher,

---

"This reading group saw no fictional Blacks, Hispanics, or Orientals for their school in a mostly white, middle-class neighborhood."

---

this was his first year as a librarian. The previous librarian at Plaza had been more "research oriented." Derrick's delight was in fiction: He loved challenging kids creatively with new words. "My kids had been asking for those Cedar Valley books," he said, "and when they saw the new C. S. Lewis books they were ready to grab them right off my counter!"

The Kansas City group gifted their school with:

- Five of Judy Baer's *Cedar Valley Daydreams* books. Bethany House.

- Jean Harmeling's *The Potter on Charles Street,* Crossway Books, 1990.

- Janette Oke's *Love's Long Journey.* Bethany House, 1983.

- Frank Peretti's *The Door in the Dragon's Throat.* Crossway, 1985.

- C. S. Lewis' *The Lion, the Witch and the Wardrobe* and *The Silver Chair.* Macmillan, 1980.

They hoped these books would add to the library's few personal-God books, and balance the high percentage of person-centered and spirit-centered books in Plaza's 12,500-book collection. They hoped their books would show a more accurate percentage of homemakers—at least higher than the 18 percent they'd found in the middle school books.

These parents plan more donations and are excited about having real input in the public schools. None of their children are old enough to read these books, but they mean to start early with their commitment to their kids' educations.

Plaza Middle School Books
Reviewed by Parent Reading Group

- Bunting, Eve. *Ghost Children*. Clarion Books, 1989.

- Conford, Ellen. *Genie With the Light Blue Hair*. Bantam, 1989.

- Cross, Gillian. *Map of Nowhere*. Holiday House, 1988.

- Duffy, James. *Cleaver of the Good Luck Diner*. Macmillan, 1989.

- Hahn, Mary Downing. *The Doll in the Garden*. Clarion, 1989.

- Haynes, Mary. *Catch the Sea*. Bradbury Press, 1989.

- Hughes, Dean. *Family Pose*. Atheneum/Macmillan, 1989.

- Kaye, Marilyn. *A Friend Like Phoebe*. Harcourt, Brace, 1987.

- Kendall, Jane. *Miranda and the Movies*. Crown Publishing, 1989.

- Kline, Suzy. *Orp*. G. P. Putnam's Sons, 1989.

- Lisle, Janet Taylor. *Afternoon of the Elves*. Orchard Books, 1989.

- Sargent, Sarah. *McFee, ATP*. Bradbury, 1989.

- Staples, Suzanne Fisher. *Shabanu*. Alfred A. Knopf, 1989.

- Towne, Mary. *Wanda, the Worry Wart*. Macmillan, 1989.

Library Revolution in Oxnard, California

When Dorothy Bearss walked through the doors of her local junior college ten years ago, she opened a whole new phase of her life.

In that college library she made a discovery: The feminist ideology was so entrenched in women's and family issues that "censorsip by ommission" prevented her from conducting balanced research. She dropped out of school for awhile and reassessed her future.

Through prayer and Bible reading she became convinced that the portion of 1 Corinthians 2:5 which says ". . . that your faith should not stand in the wisdom of men, but in the power of God" (RSV) was meant for her. If she wanted a balanced college library, *she* would have to balance it!

The college president listened sympathetically as Mrs. Bearss laid out her plea: She supported the school with her taxes. She wanted bal-

---

"In that college library she made a discovery:
The feminist ideology was so entrenched
in women's and family issues that 'censorsip
by ommission' prevented her
from conducting balanced research."

---

anced schooling—not indoctrination. She wanted books on all points of view—not just the feminist and anti-family ideology. When she offered to donate books, the president offered no resistance.

She and two friends then looked at their public library's periodical displays which promote themes like "Women's History Month" and "National Family Week."

Working far ahead of Women's History Month, they asked the library staff: Could they balance the library's stock with gift books and a display showing the homemaker's role in American history? Placed prominently, "Women's History—Another Point of View" contrasted the feminist stereotype of homemakers with the traditional roles for men and women. Their poster carefully spelled out the *real* government figures which show 61 percent of mothers of teens working less than thirty-five hours per week.

Not once have Mrs. Bearss or her friends been refused the privilege of donating library books—to date they've given eighty to one hundred books in their local community. "The positive solution to problems always means much more work," she says. She always treats librarians and newspaper people with respect, and she and her co-workers take weeks to prepare displays and read books before deciding to donate them.

She and her group send listings of every donated book to the local paper. Maybe that's why she's often quoted, and appears on TV and radio talk shows. Interviewers sometimes label her "traditionalist," "re-entry homemaker" or "kitchen lawyer." But she'd rather call herself "family and women-at-home advocate."

"I tell talk-show hosts and reporters that my biggest frustration in the college libraries was not being able to practice my freedom of speech," she states.

In her own community, where the litmus test is always toughest, she is well known as a careful researcher. One local library wanted a list of creation science publications to "balance their viewpoint." They asked Mrs. Bearss for recommendations.

The donation plan keeps Dorothy Bearss and her friends reading constantly. She asserts, "We don't donate a book unless we've read it." Do they find any "100 percent perfect" books? "No," she says. And that's what makes the library diverse.

Maybe others who've tried to copy her are holding out for that 100 percent perfection. "I've heard from more than two hundred others around the country, wanting to know how it's done," she continues. "Not all of them are successful in their own libraries. Possibly it's lack of groundwork."

Mrs. Bearss is convinced that she succeeds because of this four-fold strategy:

1. Establish credibility in your own community as a reasonable person—as someone who wants to *add* books—not ban them!
2. Organize a low-key, pro-family group. Many libraries would rather deal with groups than with individuals—this is especially true when it comes to authorizing major book displays.
3. Find out who handles library displays. Introduce yourself.
4. Find out if library officials are sympathetic towards the pro-family view. If so, use National Family Week and other related dates for book displays and donations.[3]

I am convinced that Dorothy Bearss also succeeds because each step of her plan includes courtesy and careful research.

*"It began ten years ago as a simple plan
to diversify her college library so she could
get a balanced education. But what it turned
into leaves her shaking her head
in wonder at God's power."*

It began ten years ago as a simple plan to diversify her college library so she could get a balanced education. But what it turned into leaves her shaking her head in wonder at God's power.

Would you like help with your library? If you include at least $1 to cover costs, you'll get fact sheets and encouragement from: Dorothy Bearss; Pro-Family Advocate, P.O. Box 43148, Port Hueneme, California 93043. Add another dollar and she'll send a "Motherhood Is A Proud Profession" bumper sticker.

It Isn't Easy to Walk into Your Own Library

By far my toughest days in this book project were the times I chatted with my own school librarians. My first contacts five years ago left me wondering if I could bring *any* kind of opinion to bear without hearing, "Well, of course, we don't believe in censoring anything."

So it was an overwhelming surprise five years later to face a knowledgeable, gracious town librarian willing to (a) listen to my opinions and (b) handle my gifted magazine subscription without any more challenge than wishing to know the name of the magazine and the general type.

This made it easier to read fiction from my own Cedar Falls, Iowa library shelves and make the same kind of report which the Hiawatha, Kansas City and our own national-project parent group had done. But pressed for time, I read every book and made every report myself. Therefore, I was concerned that the Cedar Falls report might not carry the same credibility or balance as the others.

However, my data were almost identical to the other four reading projects. My town library's slightly lower profanity and sexual situations (as in the Hiawatha group) once again reflected the "adult books for young adults" which were not on the young adult shelves. World-life views were almost the same—though slightly higher in the impersonal-spirits group, and tough teens who lean on anyone but parents were there for the picking.

What a great disappointment that in our mostly white community, characters in the new hardbacks which I read were mostly white. There were only tiny numbers of even *token* or *incidental* characters from other races.

Monotonous, repeated themes of good-guy white collars, negative homemakers, and bumbling clergy had me wondering if I'd mixed up the reading list with the other cities.

Once again I was overwhelmed by the seductive writing. These authors know how to nail kids to their chairs! When two teens say there are no good marriages, you believe them. When a girl disguised as a knight needs a witch's help and her lover's bed, you sympathize! When outer-space aliens perform miracle healing, you're ready to drop traditional medicine and fly to Azure.

But it is also true that when one teen commits so thoroughly to his girlfriend that his life literally hangs from the bridge, you're ready to give real commitment another chance. When a young boy loses his father on a lonely planetary outpost, you're ready to copy his gutsy discipline. And when a young Jewish girl tells you not all is well in Christian, apartheid South Africa, you believe her.

1990 New Teen Books in the Cedar Falls Library
(* These do not appear on data sheet)

- *Crutcher, Chris. *Chinese Handcuffs*. Greenwillow Books, 1989.
- Dereske, Jo. *The Lone Sentinel*. Atheneum, 1989.
- Felice, Cynthia. *Light Raid*. Ace Books. Berkley, 1989.
- Green, Connie Jordan. *The War at Home*. Margaret K. McElderry Books, 1989.
- Pierce, Tamora. *In the Hand of the Goddess*. Atheneum, 1984.
- Richardson, Jean. *Beware Beware*. Viking/Penguin, 1989.

---

*"Once again I was overwhelmed by the
seductive writing. These authors know how
to nail kids to their chairs! When two teens
say there are no good marriages,
you believe them. When a girl disguised
as a knight needs a witch's help and her
lover's bed, you sympathize!"*

- Sacks, Margaret. *Beyond Safe Boundaries*. Lodestar Books. E. P. Dutton, 1989.

- *Sleator, William. *Strange Attractions*. E. P. Dutton, 1990.

- *Staples, Suzanne Fisher. *Shabanu*. Alfred A. Knopf, 1989.

- Thesman, Jean. *Appointment with a Stranger*. Houghton Mifflin, Co., 1989.

- Thesman, Jean. *The Last April Dancers*. Houghton Mifflin, 1987.

- Yolen, Jane. *A Sending of Dragons*. Delacorte Press, 1987.

I talked to the "young adult" services director of our town library and explained my hope that she would add more personal-God centered books to increase diversity on the teen shelves. I gave her my gifts, and she promised to see "if they fit library needs."

In the city of Cedar Falls tonight, there is a librarian who is reading *In the Midst of Wolves* by Barry McGuire; *The Potter on Charles Street,* by Jean Harmeling; and *Vietnam, the Other Side of Glory,* by William Kimball. She promises me shelf space for them soon.

I love my city library. I have never been treated with anything but the greatest respect there. My kids grew up wandering its carpeted, book-lined halls. When I taught young adult literature at the Lutheran Home's mini college, our library children's director plied me with enough books to line a truck and I was told, "Don't worry about getting them all back on time." When I substituted at the local Christian elementary school, the city library became the school library on a joyful, bussed outing. When I researched flour mills, my library trusted me with a 1794 antique book on inter-library loan from Luther College.

My dear library: I thank you! Soon after many friends asked you to stock Frank Peretti's million-dollar best-sellers, they appeared in the card catalog. Peretti now stands alongside Francis Schaeffer and Charles Colson on your sturdy shelves—all of them taking their rightful places among the great thinkers of the twentieth century.

I know it will not be long before I see Mike Warnke's, Pat Pulling's, or Tipper Gore's warnings about the occult standing alongside your stock of occult phenomena. And once in at least ten times I hope a young teenager's hand will soon brush a full-bodied, God-centered novel—with some minorities as modern-day heroes! I'm looking forward to buying some of those books for you. Because I know that once you start stocking these books, you will love them, too.

8

Books to Keep

After two years of reading the forty-five books reviewed in earlier chapters, my love of literature focused more sharply: I was more than ever convinced of the lure of exquisite writing. And I was convinced that what is said exquisitely can change lives. Often in this project's forty-five books, what passed for beauty was simple fatalism wrapped up in tender packages. What promised us real problems didn't give real answers.

I wanted to put away those forty-five books and choose real books with real answers. To choose books with fathers who came back, with adults who helped kids, and the name of God as a blessing instead of a curse.

But I discovered that whereas the public library offers row upon row of person-centered or spirit-centered views, the Christian library does not always produce vivid, polished works. And whereas our project books gave blacks an eerily positive "reverse racism," Christian books rarely mentioned minorities. Whereas the project books rubbed our noses in self-centered present-day teens, the best Christian books were historical novels.

It looked as if I might have one foot in the gray world of relativism and another in mediocrity.

What I wanted was both feet in the sparkling water of life. I wanted a book that grabbed me on its first page, that made me laugh or cry "Oh yes!" and that deposited me on the opposite shore a new person. But I didn't give up my search. And I finally found those books—in the Christian bookstore.

Fourteen Great Books

Here are fourteen books your teenagers can tuck in undershirt drawers or invite to bedside tables. I close the door on a gray world of non-answers and present my gift to young people: fourteen books that can change their lives.

1. *River of Fire,* by Bettie Wilson Story (David C. Cook, 1978)

After Malinda's mother dies in their backwoods cabin, her father tearfully sends her to Mobile for more schooling. But a midnight fire scatters paddleboat passengers into the icy river. Malinda makes it to shore.

Delirious with the same fever that took her mother, she is nursed to health by a runaway slave girl. For two months they take turns saving each other from mosquitoes, wild hogs, overturned boats, and slavers. They learn to trust God for every berry and stick of firewood—and they learn to trust each other.

It's a free black family that finally sends the girls where they need to be—Malinda to Mobile and her father, and Jasmine to New York as a free black. The author's unusual dialogue skill, historical authenticity, and fast-paced narrative will put junior high readers in one quiet spot until the book is finished.

2. *This Present Darkness,* by Frank Peretti (Crossway Books, 1986)

If we could actually *see* spiritual warfare, we would faint. Peretti almost gets us there, in this unique thriller which casts two sets of characters—one spiritual, the other human.

Horrid, lizard-like demons, their sulphurous breath blotting the sky, gain ascendancy in the little town of Ashton. Their human counterparts plan a new age takeover. But where is God's power? Where are the believers? Who is praying? Peretti paints a believable answer: Angels thwart demon power and gain muscle with every human prayer.

This is a real eye opener: of the value of prayer, of demon warfare behind heavy metal music, magic crystals, and meditation. For ages fourteen and up, a million and a half copies have been sold.

> *"This is a real eye opener: of the value of prayer, of demon warfare behind heavy metal music, magic crystals, and meditation. For ages fourteen and up, a million and a half copies have been sold."*

3. *Piercing the Darkness,* by Frank Peretti (Crossway Books, 1989)

Someone wants to murder Sally Beth Roe. Run, Sally, run—from your new age past, from horrible secrets in the motel room, from being unable to trust another soul.

But Someone else is gently pulling her back. Someone else protects her from skulking, fiery demons, and a Satan-worshipping hierarchy whose list she hides.

Even more exciting than *This Present Darkness,* the story pits a minister against new age school curriculum and false child abuse claims. Peretti skillfully pulls a dozen hair-raising threads into a tightly woven, explosive ending. A million and a half copies sold. Age fourteen and up.

4. *Run Baby Run,* by Nicky Cruz with Jamie Buckingham (Bridge Publishing, New Jersey. 1968)

We made an exception to our "fiction only" rule and included this autobiography because of its Hispanic theme. Though set in the fifties, the drugs, killing, loneliness, occultism, gangs, and suicide themes are relevant today.

Raised in a Puerto Rican "spiritist" home, Nicky grew up hating and fearing both parents, who sent him to New York at age fifteen. Fleeing any kind of authority, he finds his own apartment and "earns" a living through stealing, killing, and street warfare. Soon he's the feared leader of New York's most murderous gang.

Onto this scene comes a small, skinny preacher who dares to say "I love you." The explosive climax of this meeting is so unbelievable, no fiction editor would have touched it. This true story may be a little graphic for some twelve-year-olds. But they may be safer reading it than not. Over two million copies sold. Age fourteen and up.

6. *Paco,* by John Benton (Fleming H. Revell Co., 1985)

After reading *Run Baby Run,* it's easier to believe the theme of this fast-paced street novel. Paco is caught in a web of robbery, drugs, treacherous street friends, and fly-by-night relationships.

Not as graphic or violent as Cruz's book, it's aimed at twelve to sixteen-year-olds. You may not like literature that spells out the salvation message, but it fights for attention with shelves of books which spell out occultism. Based on true events of residents of the Walter Hoving Home of Garrison, New York, and Teen Challenge of New York City. Ages twelve to sixteen.

7. *Whalesong.* by Robert Siegel (Crossway Books, 1981)

Though relevant to our "Save the Whales" society, this book isn't about saving whales.

It's about souls. Siegel's allegory is as broad as the ocean, as musical as the deepest instrument.

Hruna the whale lives an ordinary leviathan life—echoing family arias, sporting with dolphins, finding a lifelong mate, and munching on krill—the whale's staff of life. But his size and courage have marked him. One day he knows he must "take the plunge" to feed his soul and make the Great Whale Hralekana his lovesong.

This new song moves him to terrorize the dreaded whale boats: his life in exchange for his mate and his pod. "It was a fine morning on which to die," he says. But from the depths of the ocean comes someone else to die in his place—the giant whale Hralekana sings again—and this time deathsong—and resurrection. Age twelve and up.

8. *The Lion, The Witch and The Wardrobe.* by C. S. Lewis (Macmillan Publishing Co., 1980)

When four English children step into a closet wardrobe, they expect to find old coats. Instead, a forever-winter sort of place quickly involves them in a witch's cold stranglehold, animals that serve high tea, and a massive Lion's sacrificial love.

Lewis' masterful allegory and humorous dialogue have children right where he wants them—surrounded by the Master Plan of the Universe. Parents, let your children read the Narnia Books before you get hooked on them yourselves. Ages ten and up.

9. *The Great Divorce,* by C. S. Lewis (Macmillan, 1946)

If you lived in a gray, murky hell and could take a bus ride to heaven, would you go?

This short allegory packs a strange load of grumbling bus passengers on their way to a celestial surprise—where grass is sharp and falling apples dense enough to kill you.

But if you give up your heart's desires and decide to stay, something happens to your body, and grass was never more real. Suddenly, heaven is a place where rivers laugh and bold new bodies are solid enough to gaze on the most important Resident.

It's a place where you just might want to stay. Age fifteen and up.

---

*"The giant whale Hralekana sings again—
and this time deathsong—and resurrection."*

---

10. *The Incredible Journey,* by Sheila Burnford
(Bantam Skylark, 1987)

No child is too old to recognize the "lodestone of longing" in three animals who brave the Canadian wilderness for the family they love.

A prankish Siamese cat, a gentlemanly labrador retriever, and an aging bull terrier search for their western home and the children who loved them. Nearly drowned in a raging river, mauled by an outraged mother bear, and infested with porcupine quills, the three blend their skills to feed and encourage each other through three hundred miles of forest.

Burnford makes an unbelievable event sing. Her simple narrative receives the occasional metaphorical gem without straining. Age ten and up. Over three million copies in print.

11. *The Gates of Zion,* by Bodie Thoene
(Bethany House, 1986)

Bodie Thoene and husband Brock team up in this explosive historical novel for older teens. It's must reading for every history course which covers the Mid-East crisis.

This book is a romance if you're in that mood, a macho adventure if that's your diet. Or—a way to satisfy the intellectually curious and the spiritually dry.

Young American Ellie photographs her way through a brand-new Israel in 1947, immortalizing murdered Arabs, Holocaust refugees, and confused Britishers. Through this upheaval she must decide between American fighter-pilot David or the quiet, strong Moshe—a "completed" Jew. At her side is fourteen-year-old Polish refugee Yacov, who rescues her from the Mufti's henchmen.

The complicated plot will probably safeguard this book from younger teens, who might be disturbed by the somewhat graphic violence. But for those willing to drop everything and wade into 368 pages of adventure, it's well worth the journey.

Both Christian and Jew can benefit from the accurate portrayal of Hassidim, Zionist, and "completed" Jews, and Arabs who are born-again Christians. Thoene restrains her message of an eternal Messiah to a loving whisper, but it rings loud and clear.

12. *The Potter of Charles Street,* by Jean Harmeling
(Crossway Books, 1990)

On an island near Boston, Eve begins her story. She's eleven and facing puberty, a grumpy invalid father, and a promiscuous sister. She'd like to keep schoolmate Bobby as a "best friend," although father, sister, and some friends tease and threaten. When Bobby's father dies in Vietnam and his mother remarries, Bobby moves far away, creating an aching void in Eve.

While supposedly attending the hated "charm school" in Boston with her sister, she leaves the class and wanders city streets in search of sanctuary.

A potter's shop intrigues her. Through the gentle skill of a Vietnam veteran, she learns the secrets of clay. She also learns deeper truths—of

God's care, and of her father's need for love. As a balance to so many books casting nasty fathers, *The Potter* redeems the father-daughter relationship through service and forgiveness.

This book leaves Eve at age seventeen, wise to God's leading and of her need to serve. The writing is as subtle and original as Eve's "purply stone"; it glistens brightly with wetness, but fades when held too long. Age thirteen and up.

13. *In the Midst Of Wolves,* by Barry McGuire and Logan White (Crossway Books, 1990)

Writing from his biker past, Christian singer Barry McGuire tunes us in to the futility of drugs and the sheer terror of the "Harley" world.

Not at all sure he wants to end up in the "stone hotel," Backer tries to wrench himself and brother Colt away from the gang. But futility reins, and Colt kills himself.

Desperate and vicious, Backer roams the solitary hills, never expecting rescue by a black man and his two camping kids.

In the beginning, Backer doesn't appreciate the rescue—though it's Kobol's decision to keep him rescued at all costs. He drags him to Boulder, where a university professor anchors Backer in a quiet classroom, daring him not to believe in the One who made the universe.

Convinced and broken, Backer—a new man—finds the strength to confront the old Harley gang and spread his newfound peace. But it's tough sledding, and not until he's nearly hung in a Halloween ritual do some of the bikers see the real love through Backer's broken body. Brutality and gentleness war side by side in this amazingly crafted book. Rough scenes, but no profanity. Age fourteen and up.

14. *Vietnam, The Other Side of Glory,* by William R. Kimball (Ballantine Books, 1987)

At last—a true account of the spiritual dimension of that bloody war. Fourteen seasoned and raw recruits tell their emotional stories of drug abuse, horror, and grief.

But unlike most Vietnam tales, God's ability to reverse war's after-trauma is given the recognition it deserves. Told without maudlin embellishments, these stories will captivate your older teenagers. No profanity, no sexual situations. But nothing else is withheld. Age fourteen and up.

"Repressed Books": A Sampling

Author Staci Charles of Hiawatha, Kansas (see chapter 7) knew that if she could just get librarians hooked on good Christian books, they'd begin stocking them—thus restoring balance. She challenged: "If we are really going to 'separate church and state' then we will need to treat books with any atheist or agnostic statement with the same segregation that Christian books have received."

Here is her list: "A Small Sampling of Repressed Books" (I've included only the fiction).

1. Bacher, June Masters. *Love Leads Home*. Harvest House Publishers, 1984. At turn-of the century, True North leaves her Oregon home for Atlanta, Georgia, and her roots.

2. Dengler, Sandy. *Code of Honor*. Bethany House, 1988. Three sisters emigrate to Queensland, Australia to evade a dark future in turn-of-the-century Ireland.

3. Johnson, Lissa Halls. *Just Like Ice Cream*. Ronald N. Haynes Publishers, 1982. Sixteen-year-old Julie becomes pregnant in her first intimate relationship and struggles with decisions of adoption, abortion, or child-rearing.

4. Lawhead, Stephen R. *Dream Thief*. Crossway Books, 1983. It's 2043 on an American space station. Spencer Reston struggles against mind-control and an overthrow plot.

5. Morris, Gilbert. *The Honorable Imposter*. Bethany House, 1986. A spy on the Mayflower? Gilbert Winslow is hired to infiltrate religious separatists on the Mayflower and must deal with faith and doubt, good and evil.

6. Oke, Janette. *When Calls the Heart*. Bethany House, 1983. Can a cultured schoolmarm from the East brave the Canadian West and also change the mind of a bachelor-minded Canadian Mountie?

7. Oke, Janette. *Love's Unfolding Dream*. Bethany House, 1987. Book 6 in "Love Comes Softly" series. Three young women

> **"But unlike most Vietnam tales, God's ability to reverse war's after-trauma is given the recognition it deserves. Told without maudlin embellishments, these stories will rivet your older teenagers to their chairs."**

growing up together in pioneer times—they're all interested in the same man.

8. Peretti, Frank E. *The Door in the Dragon's Throat.* Crossway Books, 1985. In the Mideastern desert, Jay and Lila Cooper join their archaeologist father to penetrate a cave with mysterious powers.

9. Wells, Marian. *Colorado Gold.* Bethany House, 1988. How does a sixteen-year-old preacher's daughter on a lonely pioneer outpost know if the religious values she holds are really her own?

10. MacDonald, George. *Sir Gibbie.* E.P. Dutton and Co., Inc., 1979. Orphaned Sir Gibbie, born without speech, searches for home and identity in this nineteenth-century Scottish novel.

Appendix A: Parent's Reading Questionnaire

Reader's name _____ Date finished _____

TITLE _____ AUTHOR _____

PUBLISHER _____ YEAR _____ NO. PAGES _____

BRIEF SYNOPSIS OF STORY _____

_____

_____

_____

SETTING (time, location, place) _____

PROTAGONIST:

NAME	SEX	AGE	RACE	NATIONALITY
1.				
OTHER CHARACTERS (up to 9 others)				
2.				
3.				
4.				
5.				
6.				
7.				
8.				
9.				
10.				

PROBLEM-SOLVING TOOLS: Indicate how many characters (up to 10) used each tool by placing a numeral under the appropriate column:

P used as positive tool in the story

N used as negative tool in the story

B sometimes positive, sometimes negative, or not sure which

P	N	B		
			1.	alcohol
			2.	drugs
			3.	eating
			4.	fantasy
			5.	giving up
			6.	God
			7.	manipulation
			8.	playing the clown
			9.	reasoning
			10.	running away
			11.	situational ethics (lying)
			12.	spirit world
			13.	suicide
			14.	support from peers, siblings
			15.	support from parents
			16.	support from other adults
			17.	tobacco
			18.	verbal abuse
			19.	withdrawal, denial
			20.	undefined *forces*
			21.	vengeance
			22.	violence (physical)

RACES AND NATIONALITIES: Categorize up to 10 characters by placing the numeral under the categories "P" (positive), "N" (negative) or "B" (blend).

P	N	B	
			1. Asian American
			2. Black American
			3. Caucasian American
			4. Hispanic
			5. Native American
			6. African, Black
			7. African, Caucasian
			8. Australia, New Zealand Caucasian
			9. Australia, New Zealand native
			10. European
			11. Middle European
			12. Mideastern
			13. Oriental
			14. Indian
			15. Fictional or outer space
			16. Other

AGE RANGE: How many characters (up to 10) in each category? How portrayed?

NUMBER		POSITIVE	NEGATIVE	A BLEND
____	Infants			
____	Pre-schoolers			
____	Elementary (5-11)			
____	Teenagers (12-18)			
____	Young Adults (19-35)			
____	Middle-age (36-55)			
____	Older			

AUTHORITY FIGURES: Categorize up to 10 characters.
How are they portrayed?

NUMBER	POSITIVE	NEGATIVE	A BLEND
_____ Government (any)			
_____ Clergy			
_____ Peace-keeping officials			
_____ School administrators			
_____ Teachers			
_____ Organizational leaders			

HANDICAPS: Do any characters (up to 10) have physical
or mental handicaps? How are the people with these
handicaps portrayed?

	POSITIVE	NEGATIVE	A BLEND
Character _____ Handicap			
Character _____ Handicap			
Character _____ Handicap			
Character _____ Handicap			

LANGUAGE AND STYLE: Was the language SUITABLE
to the story? (Characters spoke in their own language,
accurately representing their situation and era),
NOT SUITABLE (Characters used language
inappropriate to their situation), or A BLEND?

_____ SUITABLE _____ NOT SUITABLE _____ A BLEND

Did use or lack of profanity, vulgarities or obscenities
influence your reading?

_____ POSITIVELY _____ NEGATIVELY _____ A BLEND

Profanities, vulgarities, and obscenities represented

_____ None of the language _____ Occasional reference
_____ Frequent reference   _____ Continual reference

SEXUAL EXPRESSION: (This category replaces a more
complicated "Relationship" category in our "Project-45")

The author appeared to approve of sexual intercourse
outside of heterosexual marriage

STRONGLY _____ SOMEWHAT _____

Not approve of sexual intercouse outside of
heterosexual marriage

STRONGLY _____ SOMEWHAT _____

Sexual intercourse was not mentioned _____

WOMEN'S AND MEN'S ROLES: You may choose more than
one role for each character. Characterize up to 10 people.
Check "P" (Positive), "N" (Negative) or "B" (A Blend)
beside the role.

P	N	B	
			father
			husband
			mother
			wife
			student
			blue collar
			homemaker
			civic or religious volunteer work
			pink collar (secretarial or other professional support work)
			professional, white collar
			self-employed
			unemployed
			wandering from job to job

WOMEN'S AND MEN'S ROLES IN COMBINATION:
Indicate how many of these characters had
combined roles:

Number of Characters   Combined Role

_____   Mother/employment
_____   Student/employment
_____   Father/employment

WORLD-LIFE VIEWS: Which world-life views are represented?
Choose one or more. Check number value beside each view:
1.   No indication
2.   Occasional reference
3.   Frequent reference
4.   Continual reference
Also indicate whether these views were portrayed as
POSITIVE, NEGATIVE, or A BLEND.

	1	2	3	4	P	N	B
Impersonal spirit or gods-centered life view. Gods or spirits are indifferent or hostile - need to be placated or manipulated.							
Friendly spirit-centered. Humorous, capricious, or supportive spirit, having little power or capricious power.							
Personal God. Life view centered on one, all-powerful God who created the world and is lovingly involved with His creatures.							
Object-centered life view. Fate or undefined *forces* sometimes or always control life.							
Person-centered life view. People have increasing ability to solve problems without outside interference or help.							

RECOMMENDATIONS: If you were to recommend this book to your teenager, how would you do it? Check one or more:

1. Read it together and discuss it with him/her.
2. Suggest she/he read it alone.
3. Ask him/her to read it and make list of questions.
4. Purchase the book for him/her so she/he will re-read it.
5. Recommend other books to be read in conjunction._____

6. Do not recommend.

LITERARY IMPACT: At the end of the book, did the sum total of your reading leave you (check one or more)

1. confused
2. depressed
3. finding positive new ways to solve problems.
4. hopeful
5. hopeless
6. laughing
7. questioning
8. resenting individuals or groups
9. romantically inclined
10. sexually inclined
11. understanding people in a new or better way
12. disappointed
13. worried or fearful
14. angry

Appendix B: "Project-45" Findings in Graphs

Graph 1: Literary impact

The book left me feeling:

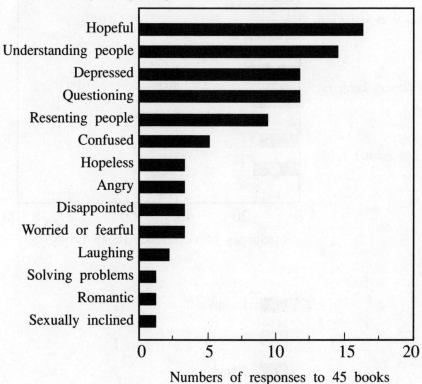

Numbers of responses to 45 books

Graph 2: World-life views

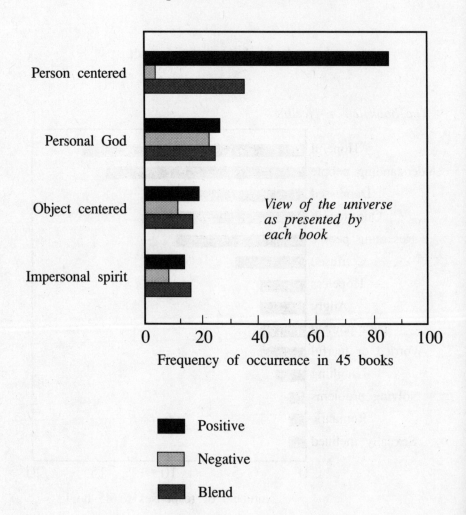

Person centered

Personal God

Object centered

Impersonal spirit

View of the universe as presented by each book

0   20   40   60   80   100

Frequency of occurrence in 45 books

■ Positive

▨ Negative

▨ Blend

Graph 3: Relationships among characters

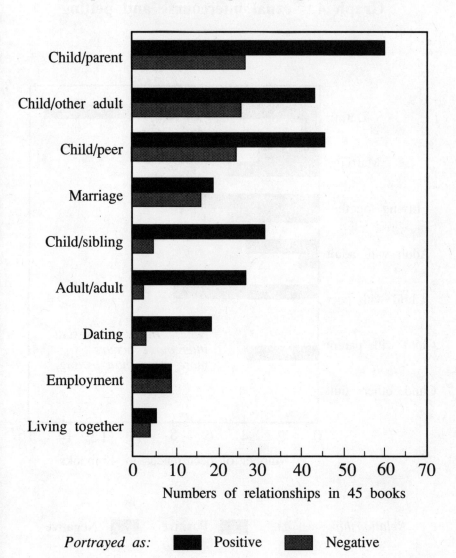

Numbers of relationships in 45 books

Portrayed as: Positive Negative

Graph 4: Sexual intercourse and petting

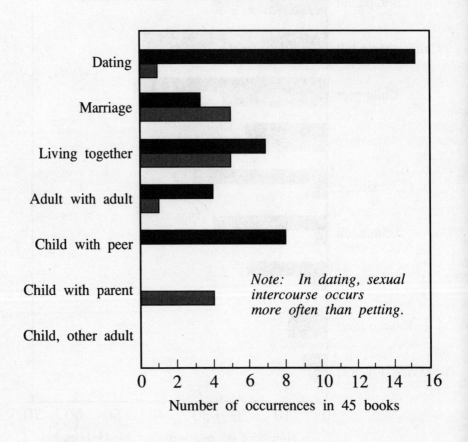

Note: In dating, sexual intercourse occurs more often than petting.

Relationship seen as: ■ Positive ▨ Negative

Graph 5: Committment in relationships

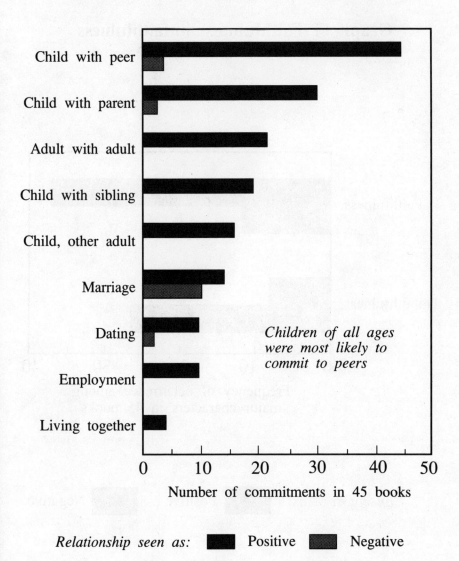

Relationship seen as: ■ Positive ▨ Negative

Graph 6: Faithfulness, unfaithfulness in marriage relationships

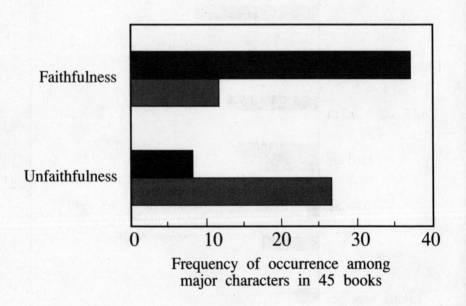

Frequency of occurrence among
major characters in 45 books

Graph 7: Authority figures

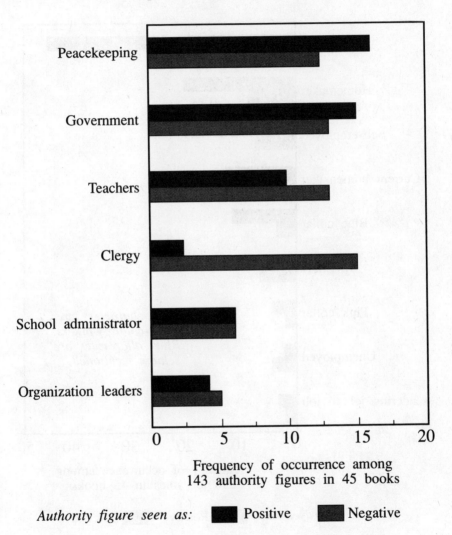

Frequency of occurrence among
143 authority figures in 45 books

Authority figure seen as: Positive   Negative

Graph 8: Jobs of women and men

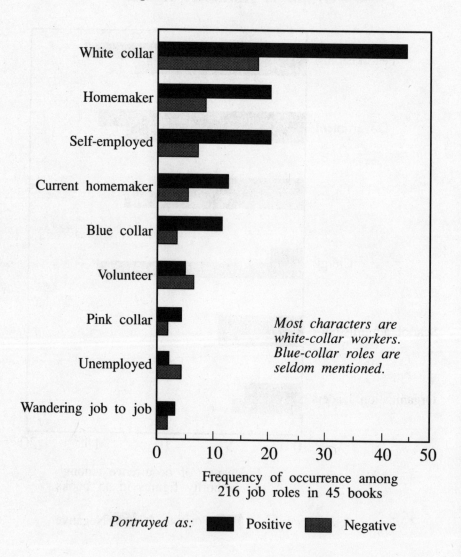

Most characters are
white-collar workers.
Blue-collar roles are
seldom mentioned.

Frequency of occurrence among
216 job roles in 45 books

Portrayed as: ■ Positive   ▨ Negative

Graph 9: Roles of women and men ranked in order of *positive* portrayal

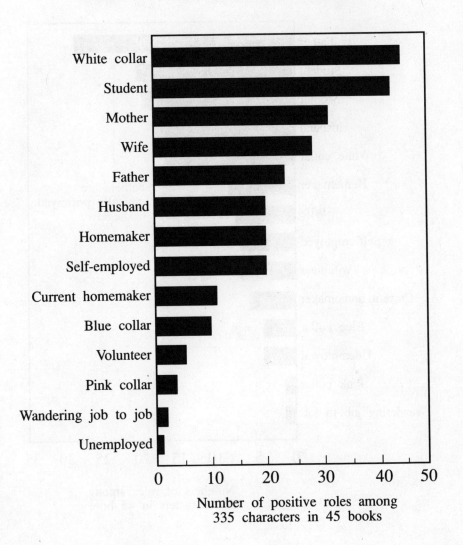

Number of positive roles among
335 characters in 45 books

Graph 10: *Negative* roles of women and men

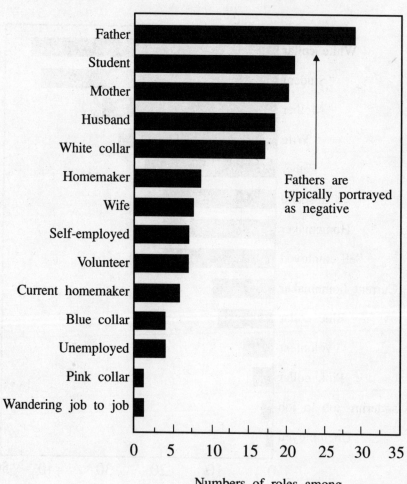

Fathers are typically portrayed as negative

Numbers of roles among
335 characters in 45 books

Graph 11: Death of one or personal enemy experienced by a major character

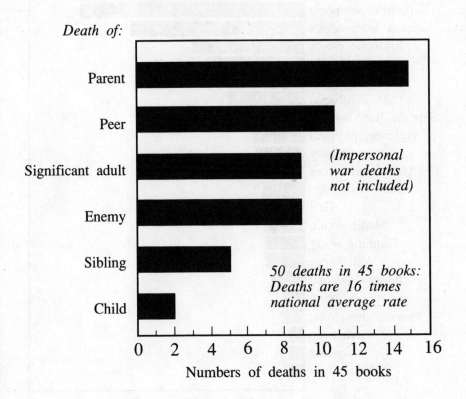

Death of:

Parent

Peer

Significant adult

Enemy

Sibling

Child

(Impersonal war deaths not included)

50 deaths in 45 books: Deaths are 16 times national average rate

0   2   4   6   8   10   12   14   16

Numbers of deaths in 45 books

Graph 12: Problem solving tools portrayed as *positive* when used by major characters

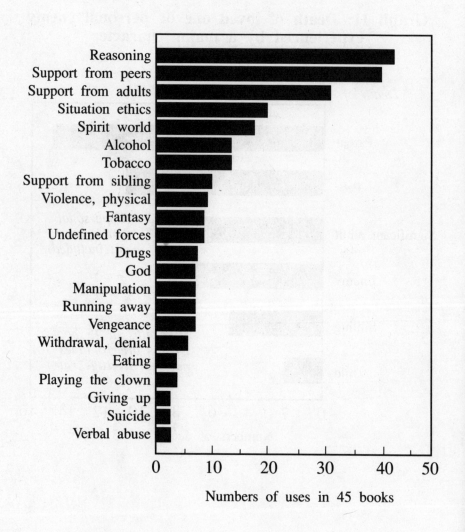

Numbers of uses in 45 books

Graph 13: Problem solving tools portrayed as *negative* when used by major characters

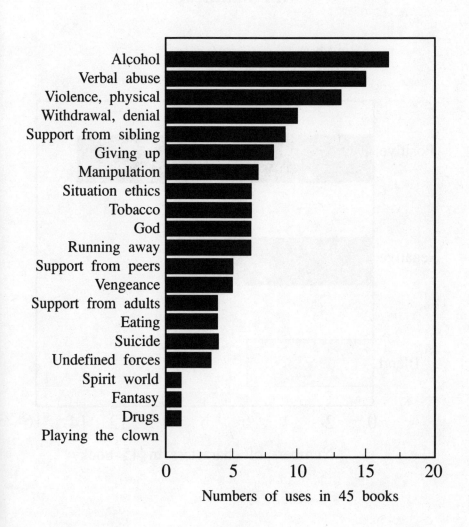

Numbers of uses in 45 books

Graph 14: Portrayal of characters with handicaps

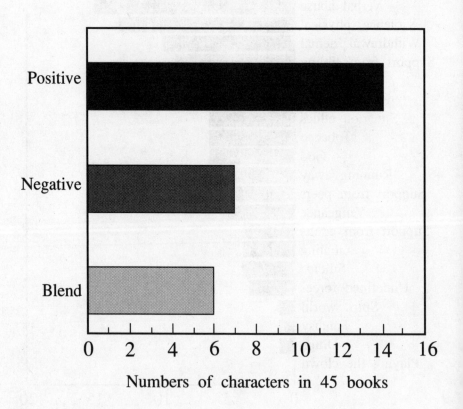

Numbers of characters in 45 books

Graph 15: Number of protagonists (lead characters) by race

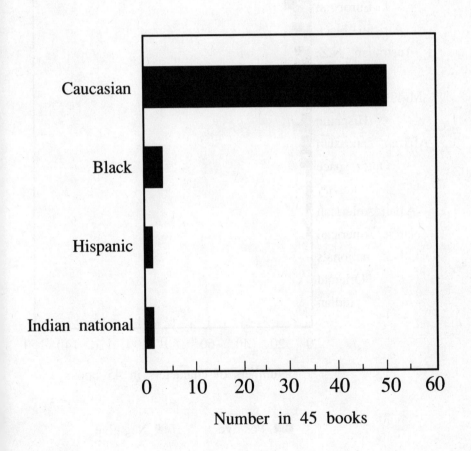

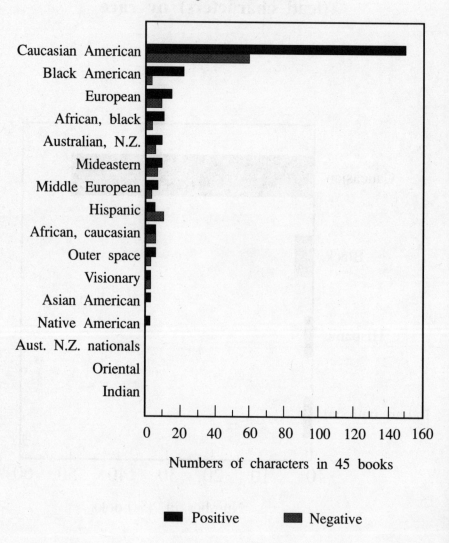

Graph 16: Race or nationality of all major characters

Caucasian American
Black American
European
African, black
Australian, N.Z.
Mideastern
Middle European
Hispanic
African, caucasian
Outer space
Visionary
Asian American
Native American
Aust. N.Z. nationals
Oriental
Indian

0   20   40   60   80   100   120   140   160

Numbers of characters in 45 books

■ Positive   ■ Negative

Graph 17: Language used by author

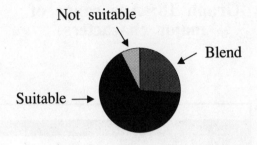

Suitability to story

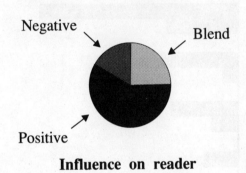

Influence on reader

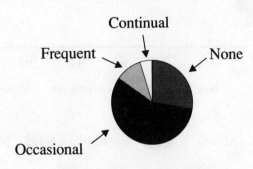

Frequency of profanity

Graph 18: Age range of major characters

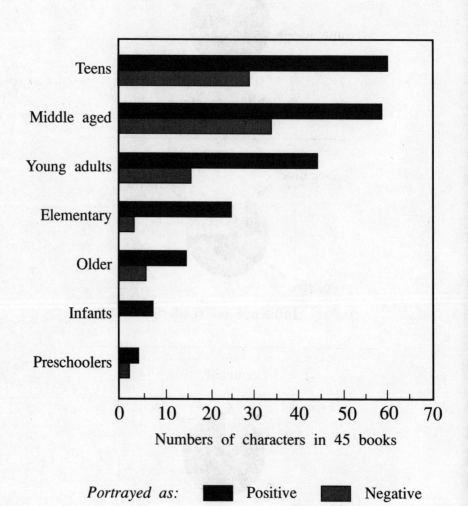

Numbers of characters in 45 books

Portrayed as: ■ Positive   ▨ Negative

Graph 19: Time setting of books

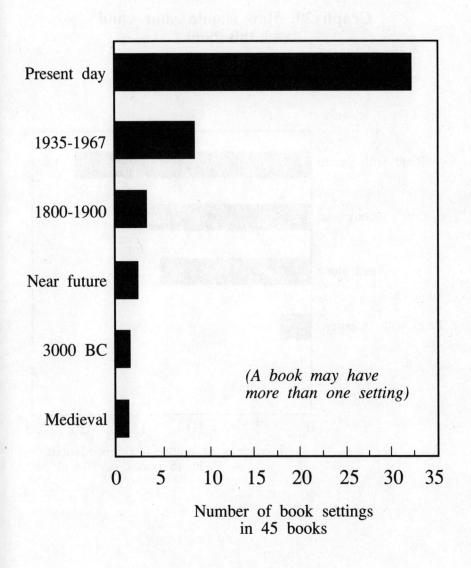

*(A book may have
more than one setting)*

Number of book settings
in 45 books

Graph 20: How should your child read this book?

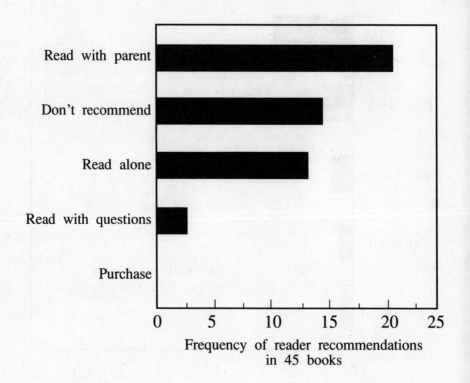

Frequency of reader recommendations
in 45 books

Appendix C: Findings from Ohio, Missouri, Kansas, and Iowa

DATA FROM BRIGGS HIGH SCHOOL, COLUMBUS, OHIO

Fifteen books read by three readers

Race of main characters and how author portrays them

	NUMBERS OF MAIN CHARACTERS			PERCENTAGE IN EACH CATEGORY		
	Positive	*Negative*	*Blend*	*Positive*	*Negative*	*Blend*
Caucasian	67	17	26	61%	15%	24%
Black	10	0	2	83%	0%	17%
Oriental	1	0	0	100%	0%	0%
Native American	1	0	0	100%	0%	0%
Hispanic	1	0	1	50%	0%	50%
Totals	**80**	**17**	**29**	**63%**	**13%**	**23%**

Author's view of sexual activity outside marriage

	Strongly	*Somewhat*	*Wasn't mentioned*
Author approves	5	3	5
Author disapproves	0	2	0

How authors portray roles of main characters

	NUMBERS OF MAIN CHARACTERS			PERCENTAGE IN EACH CATEGORY		
	Positive	*Negative*	*Blend*	*Positive*	*Negative*	*Blend*
Father	5	12	9	19%	46%	35%
Husband	4	8	5	24%	47%	29%
Mother	5	12	5	23%	55%	23%
Wife	4	5	6	27%	33%	40%
Student	32	8	6	70%	17%	13%
Blue collar	3	2	0	60%	40%	0%
Homemaker	2	7	2	18%	64%	18%
Volunteer	0	0	0	0%	0%	0%
Pink collar	1	0	0	100%	0%	0%
White collar	17	2	4	74%	9%	17%
Self-employed	5	0	7	42%	0%	58%
Unemployed	0	1	0	0%	100%	0%
Wandering job to job	1	1	0	50%	50%	0%
Totals	**79**	**58**	**44**	**44%**	**32%**	**24%**

World-life view of author

	FREQUENCY OF OCCURRENCE			PERCENTAGE IN EACH CATEGORY		
	Positive	*Negative*	*Blend*	*Positive*	*Negative*	*Blend*
Events controlled by...						
Impersonal spirit	9	0	5	64%	0%	36%
Loving personal God	3	2	2	43%	29%	29%
Fate	13	0	16	45%	0%	55%
People	38	0	4	90%	0%	10%
Totals	**63**	**2**	**27**	**68%**	**2%**	**29%**

DATA FROM HIAWATHA, KANSAS PARENT READING GROUP

Eighteen books read by five parents

Race of main characters and how author portrays them

	NUMBERS OF MAIN CHARACTERS			PERCENTAGE IN EACH CATEGORY		
	Positive	*Negative*	*Blend*	*Positive*	*Negative*	*Blend*
Caucasian	68	5	51	55%	4%	41%
Black	8	0	0	100%	0%	0%
Outer space aliens	3	1	1	60%	20%	20%
Oriental	8	4	0	67%	33%	0%
Native American	3	0	0	100%	0%	0%
Hispanic	2	1	0	67%	33%	0%
Totals	**92**	**11**	**52**	**59%**	**7%**	**34%**

Author's view of sexual activity outside marriage

	Strongly	*Somewhat*	*Wasn't mentioned*
Author approves	2	4	7
Author disapproves	1	4	0

How authors portray roles of main characters

	NUMBERS OF MAIN CHARACTERS			PERCENTAGE IN EACH CATEGORY		
	Positive	*Negative*	*Blend*	*Positive*	*Negative*	*Blend*
Father	8	4	7	42%	21%	37%
Husband	4	4	4	33%	33%	33%
Mother	10	5	8	43%	22%	35%
Wife	10	4	5	53%	21%	26%
Student	26	3	7	72%	8%	19%
Blue collar	18	1	3	82%	5%	14%
Homemaker	6	2	2	60%	20%	20%
Volunteer	5	0	0	100%	0%	0%
Pink collar	0	0	0	0%	0%	0%
White collar	13	1	2	81%	6%	13%
Self-employed	6	1	3	60%	10%	30%
Unemployed	1	3	2	17%	50%	33%
Wandering job to job	2	0	1	67%	0%	33%
Totals	**109**	**28**	**44**	**60%**	**15%**	**24%**

World-life view of author

	FREQUENCY OF OCCURRENCE			PERCENTAGE IN EACH CATEGORY		
	Positive	*Negative*	*Blend*	*Positive*	*Negative*	*Blend*
Events controlled by...						
Impersonal spirit	5	0	4	56%	0%	44%
Loving personal God	16	0	3	84%	0%	16%
Fate	0	2	9	0%	18%	82%
People	31	2	15	65%	4%	31%
Totals	**52**	**4**	**31**	**60%**	**5%**	**36%**

DATA FROM KANSAS CITY, MISSOURI
PARENT READING GROUP

Fourteen books read by five parents

Race of main characters and how author portrays them

	NUMBERS OF MAIN CHARACTERS			PERCENTAGE IN EACH CATEGORY		
	Positive	Negative	Blend	Positive	Negative	Blend
Caucasian American	74	11	16	73%	11%	16%
Black	0	0	0	0%	0%	0%
Outer space aliens	1	0	0	100%	0%	0%
Pakistani	8	1	4	62%	8%	31%
Caucasian European	4	2	4	40%	20%	40%
Middle European	1	0	0	100%	0%	0%
Totals	**88**	**14**	**24**	**70%**	**11%**	**19%**

Author's view of sexual activity outside marriage

	Strongly	Somewhat	Wasn't mentioned
Author approves	0	1	11
Author disapproves	1	1	0

How authors portray roles of main characters

	NUMBERS OF MAIN CHARACTERS			PERCENTAGE IN EACH CATEGORY		
	Positive	Negative	Blend	Positive	Negative	Blend
Father	7	6	4	41%	35%	24%
Husband	7	4	2	54%	31%	15%
Mother	7	6	6	37%	32%	32%
Wife	8	4	4	50%	25%	25%
Student	20	2	4	77%	8%	15%
Blue collar	9	0	0	100%	0%	0%
Homemaker	5	5	1	45%	45%	9%
Volunteer	1	2	0	33%	67%	0%
Pink collar	1	0	1	50%	0%	50%
White collar	8	4	1	62%	31%	8%
Self-employed	13	3	4	65%	15%	20%
Unemployed	0	1	1	0%	50%	50%
Wandering job to job	0	1	0	0%	100%	0%
Totals	**86**	**38**	**28**	**57%**	**25%**	**18%**

World-life view of author

	FREQUENCY OF OCCURRENCE			PERCENTAGE IN EACH CATEGORY		
	Positive	Negative	Blend	Positive	Negative	Blend
Events controlled by...						
Impersonal spirit	12	0	11	52%	0%	48%
Loving personal God	8	6	0	57%	43%	0%
Fate	6	0	6	50%	0%	50%
People	28	0	6	82%	0%	18%
Totals	**54**	**6**	**23**	**65%**	**7%**	**28%**

DATA FROM NINE NEW YOUNG ADULT BOOKS AT CEDAR FALLS, IOWA, LIBRARY

Race of main characters and how author portrays them

	NUMBERS OF MAIN CHARACTERS			PERCENTAGE IN EACH CATEGORY		
	Positive	Negative	Blend	Positive	Negative	Blend
Caucasian American	42	14	9	65%	22%	14%
Black	3	0	1	75%	0%	25%
Outer space aliens	3	0	9	25%	0%	75%
India	2	0	0	100%	0%	0%
Totals	**50**	**14**	**19**	**60%**	**17%**	**23%**

Author's view of sexual activity outside marriage

	Strongly	Somewhat	Wasn't mentioned
Author approves	1	2	6
Author dsapproves		1	

How authors portray roles of main characters

	NUMBERS OF MAIN CHARACTERS			PERCENTAGE IN EACH CATEGORY		
	Positive	Negative	Blend	Positive	Negative	Blend
Father	6	2	2	60%	20%	20%
Husband	1	1	2	25%	25%	50%
Mother	5	2	2	56%	22%	22%
Wife	2	1	4	29%	14%	57%
Student	10	4	4	56%	22%	22%
Blue collar	1	6	0	14%	86%	0%
Homemaker	2	1	1	50%	25%	25%
Volunteer	2	0	0	100%	0%	0%
Pink collar	2	0	0	100%	0%	0%
White collar	12	3	1	75%	19%	6%
Self-employed	2	1	2	40%	20%	40%
Unemployed	0	1	0	0%	100%	0%
Wandering job to job	0	1	0	0%	100%	0%
Totals	**45**	**23**	**18**	**52%**	**27%**	**21%**

World-life view of author

	FREQUENCY OF OCCURRENCE			PERCENTAGE IN EACH CATEGORY		
	Positive	Negative	Blend	Positive	Negative	Blend
Events controlled by...						
Impersonal spirit	17	0	2	89%	0%	11%
Loving personal God	2	6	2	20%	60%	20%
Fate	5	0	7	42%	0%	58%
People	14	0	4	78%	0%	22%
Totals	**38**	**6**	**15**	**64%**	**10%**	**25%**

Notes

Chapter 1: What Has Happened to Teen Fiction?

1. Eden Ross Lipson, *The New York Times' Parent's Guide to the Best Books for Children* (New York: Times Books, 1988).
2. Kenneth L. Donelson and Alleen Pace Nilsen, *Literature for Today's Young Adults*, 3rd ed. (New York: Scott, Foresman and Co., 1989, 1985, 1980).
3. "MacNeil/Lehrer News Hour," (May 3, 1989).
4. "Teaching Our Kids to Think," Barbara Walters' ABC Special (May 4, 1989).
5. *The Federal Register*, (September 6, 1984).

Chapter 2: How Do Books Get in the Library?

1. Glenda Tennant Neff, ed. *1990 Writer's Market*, (Cincinnati, Ohio: Writer's Digest Books, 1989).
2. Alleen Pace Nilsen and Kenneth L. Donelson, *Literature for Today's Young Adults*, (New York: Scott, Foresman and Co., 1985), 618–620.
3. Mark I. West, "Censorship in Children's Books," *Publishers Weekly*, July 24, 1987, 109.
4. Donald R. Gallo, ed., *Books for You* (Urbana, Il: National Council of Teachers of English, 1985), 284.
5. Ibid., 117.
6. *Booklist*, (March 15, 1988), 1244.
7. "Best Books for Young Adults, 1987," *Booklist*. Reproduced with permission of the American Library Association, (March 15, 1988); © 1988 ALA.
8. *School Library Journal*, (December, 1987), 35.
9. Ibid., 37–40. Reprinted with permission.

10. Ibid.

11. *Iowa Teen Award 1987–88 Masterlist,* Iowa Educational Media Association.

12. "1987 Books for Young Adults Poll," (University of Iowa), *English Journal* (January, 1988), 98–101. Copyright © 1988 by the National Council of Teachers of English. Reprinted with permission.

13. "Young Adult Editors' Choice '87," *Booklist,* 855. Reproduced with permission of the American Library Association (January 15, 1988); copyright © 1988 ALA.

14. Ibid., 855–856. Reproduced with permission of the American Library Association, copyright © 1988 ALA.

15. Interview with Kathy Jacobs, Marketing Director, Crossway Books, Westchester, Ill. January 24, 1991.

16. Interview with Jeanie Mikkelson, Bethany House Publishers, Minneapolis. January 25, 1991.

17. Paul C. Vitz, *Evidence of Bias in Our Children's Textbooks,* (Ann Arbor, Mich: Servant Books, 1986), Bryce Christensen, "Appendix B," 122.

18. Cal Thomas, *Book Burning* (Westchester, Ill.: Crossway Books, 1983), 104.

19. Ibid., 106.

20. Ibid.

21. Kathleen Baxter, "On Selecting Christian Books," *School Library Journal* (March, 1985), 118–119. Reprinted by permission.

22. Ibid.

23. Ibid.

24. Staci Charles (edited by Daisy Maryls). "Have Christian Books Been Censored?" *Publishers Weekly,* (March 3, 1989), 58.

25. Ibid.

26. Marion Dane Bauer, "The Censor Within," *Top of the News,* (Fall, 1984) 67–71.

27. *Information Power: The Library Bill of Rights* (Chicago: American Library Association and the Association for Educational Communications and Technology, 1988), 140.

28. Interviews with Connie Espel, district librarian, Princeton, Illinois School District: May and November, 1989.

29. *Library Acquisitions, Policies and Procedures,* Elizabeth Futas, ed., (Phoenix: Oryx Press, 1977), 65.

30. "Colorado Teacher Fights to have Bible Returned to Classroom," *Concerned Women for America Magazine* (February, 1989), 18–19.

31. Ibid.

32. Ibid. (February, 1991), 9.

33. Quoted in Thomas, *Book Burning,* 90.

34. *Information Power*, 140.

35. Ibid., 146.

36. Michael Scott Cain, "Censorship by the Religious Right Undermines Education," *Censorship: Opposing Viewpoints* (Greenhaven Press, St. Paul, Minn, 1985), 145.

37. *Library Journal.* ALA. June 1, 1990, p. 111.

38. Cain, "Censorship by the Religious Right," 148.

39. "Mightly Mouse: The New Adventures," *Parents Choice,* (1988 Awards Issue, November 11, 1988), 41.

40. Poll of 50 randomly selected Iowa school districts conducted by our parent reading group, May, 1988.

41. Conversation with Jay Ruckdaschel, Association of School Boards of South Dakota, July, 1989.

42. *The Education Reporter*, Alton, Illinois. March, June and November, 1988.

43. Kathleen Baxter, "On Selecting Christian Books," *School Library Journal* (March, 1985), 119. Copyright © 1985 by Reed Publishing, USA. Reprinted by permission.

Chapter 3: What We Found, Cover to Cover

1. National Council of Teachers of English, *Virginia English Bulletin* (Winter, 1984), 4 and 7.

2. Diane Ravitch and Chester E. Finn, Jr., *What Do Our 17-year-olds Know?* (New York: Harper and Row, 1987), 10.

3. Nancy Larrick, *A Parent's Guide to Children's Reading* (Philadelphia, Penn.: Westminster Press, 1982), 136.

4. Alleen Pace Nilsen and Kenneth L. Donelson, *Literature for Today's Young Adults* (New York: Scott, Foresman and Co., 1985), 81.

5. Ibid., 80.

6. Larrick, *A Parent's Guide to Children's Reading*, 136.

7. Scott Williams, "TV Smokers May Send Cloudy Message," *Waterloo Courier* (November 7, 1990), B-4.

8. Dilys Evans, "The YA Cover Story," *Publishers Weekly* (July 24, 1987), 112.

9. Ibid., 113.

10. Patrick Johnstone, *Operation World* (England and USA: STL Books, 1978), 435.

11. "All About Television," CBS 60 Minutes (July 9, 1989), transcript, 12–16.

12. Scott Williams, "TV Smokers May Send Cloudy Message," *Waterloo Courier* (November 7, 1990), B-4.

13. Jean Ferris, *Invincible Summer,* (Farrar/Straus/Giroux, 1987), 167.

14. Daniel B. Wood, "Redrawing US Portrait of Disabled," *Christian Science Monitor* (March 1, 1989), 14.

15. Kaye Gibbons, *Ellen Foster* (Vintage Books edition, 1988), 80.

16. Paul Vitz, *Evidence of Bias in Our Children's Textbooks*, 76.

17. Phyllis Schlafly, "Who's Minding the Kids," *The Phyllis Schlafly Report,* May, 1988.

18. Alvin Toffler, *Future Shock* (New York: Bantam Books, 1970), 242.

19. Bernard Goldberg, "Television Insults Men, Too," *Reader's Digest* (June, 1989), 185–6.

20. Mark I. West, "Censorship in Children's Books," *Publishers Weekly* (July 24, 1987), 109.

21. Ibid., 108–109.

22. Nilsen and Donelson, *Literature for Today's Young Adults* (609–617, Appendix A for 1985; 562–573 for 1989).

23. Quoted in Robert Marquand, "Writing an American Epic," *Christian Science Monitor* (February 3, 1989), 12.

24. J. Alfred Smith, "The Invisible Church," *Christianity Today* (March 3, 1989), 32.

25. *American Family Association Journal* (September, 1989), 1, 24.

26. Conversation with Ted Veers of the Sudan Interior Mission, former missionary to Ethiopia, October 10, 1989.

27. Wing Ning Pang, quoted in *Christianity Today* (March 3, 1989), 29.

28. John Maracle, "The Lost Nations," *Christianity Today* (March 3, 1989), 35.

29. Hadley Irwin, *Abby, My Love* (New York: Margaret K. McElderry Books, an imprint of MacMillan Pub. Co., 1985), 49. Reprinted with permission.

30. Josephine Humphreys, *Rich in Love* (Viking Penguin, Inc., 1987), 175.

31. Ibid., 77.

32. Steve Hallman, "Christianity and Humanism," *National Federation for Decency* (Tupelo, Miss., 1984), 6.

33. *Publishers Weekly* (July 24, 1987), 134.

34. Otto R. Salassi, *Jimmy D., Sidewinder, and Me* (Greenwillow Books, 1987), 48. Reprinted by permission, William Morrow and Co., Inc.

35. Ibid., 102.

36. Cynthia Voight, *Sons from Afar* (Atheneum Publishers, 1987), 138. Reprinted with permission.

37. Tipper Gore, *Raising PG Kids in an X-Rated Society* (Nashville, TN: Abingdon Press, 1987), 113.

38. Pat Pulling, *The Devil's Web* (Lafayette, La.: Huntington House, 1989).

39. Harry Mazer, *When the Phone Rang* (Scholastic, 1985), 157. Reprinted with permission.

40. Liz Hamlin, *I Remember Valentine* (Penguin Books, Inc., 1987), 19.

41. Annette Lawson, *Adultery* (New York: Basic Books Inc., 1988), 36.

42. Bryce Christensen quoting O'Connor in Vitz, *Evidence of Bias in our Children's Textbooks*, 124–125.

43. Daniel Evan, quoted by Lloyd Shearer in "Intelligence Report," *Parade Magazine* (October 1, 1989), 24.

44. Alice Dalgliesh, "New Books for Vacation Reading," *Parents' Magazine* (June, 1941), 37.

45. Ravitch and Finn, *What Do Our 17-Year-Olds Know?*, 91.

46. Interview with Pastor John Deines, Lutheran Student Center, University of Northern Iowa, August 1988.

47. Ellen Conford, *Strictly for Laughs* (Berkley/Pacer Books, 1985), 62.

48. Foundation of Literacy Project, quoted in Ravitch and Finn, 38.

Chapter 5: Don't Yell "Censor" in a Quiet Library

1. "Religion Finds Its Seat in the Classroom," *Christianity Today* (July 15, 1988), 42.

2. People For The American Way, *Attacks on the Freedom to Learn* (Washington, D. C., August 30, 1989).

3. May Hill Arbuthnot, *Children and Books* (Chicago: Scott Foresman and Co., 1964), 650.

4. Ibid., 455.

5. Richard J. Neuhaus quoted by Cal Thomas, "Court More Supportive of Religious Expression," *Waterloo Courier* (June 10, 1990), E1.

6. Will Durant, *The Story of Civilization: Part II* (New York: Simon and Schuster, 1939), 523.

7. National Education Association. *Reports of Committees, 1989–90*. Presented to 69th Representatives Association of the National Education Association, Kansas City, Mo., July 5–8.

8. *Columbia Encyclopedia*. ed William Bridgewater and Seymour Kurtz, 3rd edition, (New York and London: Columbia University Press, 1963), 466.

9. *The Iowa School Board Member,* Iowa Association of School Boards, 1986–87, 63, 64.

10. Ibid., 59.

11. "Textbook Selection: A Matter of Local Choice," Position Paper of the New York State School Boards Association (Albany, New York, 1988), 13–15.

12. Ibid., 7, 13.

13. Onalee McGraw, "Liberals Are the Book Banners," Moral Majority Report (February, 1983), 7.

14. "A Matter of Local Choice," New York Position Paper, 7.

15. Nilsen and Donelson, *Literature for Today's Young Adults*, 448.

16. Phil Riske, "Grinnell School Board Puts Vonnegut on 'Restriction,'" *Des Moines Register* (November 17, 1977).

17. *Smith v. Board of School Com'rs of Mobile County,* 655 F Supp. 939, S. D. Ala. 1987, 950.

18. Terry C. Muck, "God and Man in Buffalo," *Christianity Today* (January 13, 1989), 23.

19. *Smith v. Board*, 960.

20. Ibid., 970.

21. Ibid., 971.

22. Ibid., 980–982.

23. "A Courtroom Clash Over Textbooks," *Time* Magazine (October 27, 1986), 94.

24. Mark I. West, *Trust Your Children* (New York, London: Neal-Schuman Publishers, 1988), xii-xiii.

25. *Smith v. Board*, 947.

26. Ibid., 958.

27. *American Family Association Journal* (April, 1989), 20–21.

28. William Kirk Kilpatrick, *The Emperor's New Clothes* (Westchester, Ill.: Crossway Books, 1985), 133.

29. Ibid, chapter 11.

30. *Smith v. Board*, 957.

31. *Dimensions*, Seventh Grade Reader (Chicago: Scott, Foresman and Co., 1967), 446–7.

32. Ibid., 417.

33. Ibid., 460.

34. Conversation with Jeff Taylor, former West Virginia middle school teacher. Warsaw, In., May 17, 1989.

35. Ravitch and Finn, *What Do Our 17-Year-Olds Know?*

36. Harriet Bernstein, The Council on Basic Education, "Behind the Move to Ban More Books," *Changing Times* (June, 1982), 18.

37. Michael Farris, General Legal Counsel for Moral Majority, *Changing Times*, 21.

38. Richard Flaste, "Author Adopts Frank Kid's Book Approach to 'Tell It Like It Is,'" *New York Times* article reprinted in *The Cedar Falls, Iowa Record (October 5, 1976)*, 9.

39. U. S. Supreme Court, quoted in "Board Ends Ban on Nine Books," *St. Louis Post Dispatch (August 15, 1982)*.

40. Polly Berends, "From the Library," *Growing Child* (March, 1982), 2.

41. Steve Allen. International Paper Company ad, 1980.

42. "Dear Abby," *Waterloo Courier* (April 24, 1985), B5.

43. Wayne DeMouth, guest editorialist, "If *Grapes of Wrath* Isn't Taught in Schools, It May Disappear," *The Des Moines Register* (March 5, 1980).

44. Quote from Jeannette Eyerly in Patricia Cooney, "Kid Books: Eye-Openers For Adults," *The Des Moines Register* (June, 1980).

45. Quote from Judy Allyn. Ibid.

46. Susan Weaver, "How to Pick the Right Kids' Books," *The Des Moines Register* (November 21, 1982).

47. Margaret Clark, Children's Department of Bodley Head Publishers, London, speaking of *Little Black Sambo*. Reprinted in *Waterloo Courier* (January 28, 1986).

48. Brie Quinby, "Nancy Drew, at 50, Is Still the Top Bubble Gumshoe," *Family Weekly* (August 3, 1980), 15.

49. Bob Swift, "Advice to Parents: Let Them Read Trash," *The Des Moines Sunday Register* (March 24, 1985).

50. Nat Hentoff, special to the Washington Post, "Open Season on Books for the Young." Reprinted in *Waterloo Courier* (November 25, 1984).

51. Elizabeth Futas, ed., Edwin A. Bemis Public Library Statement, *Library Acquisition Policies and Procedures* (Phoeniz, Ariz.: Oryx Press, 1977), 59.

52. "Intellectual Freedom Manual," Statement 7b, quoted in Ibid., xi.

Chapter 6: What You Can Do

1. Vitz, *Evidence of Bias in Our Children's Textbooks*, 122, Appendix B.

2. James Baldwin, *Baldwin's Readers: Sixth and Seventh Grades Combined* (New York: American Book Co., 1897), 3.

3. Walt Whitman, *Leaves of Grass and Selected Prose* (New York: Random House Modern Library edition, 1950), 510.

4. Samuel Blumenfeld, *NEA: Trojan Horse in America*, Oklahoma City, Okla: Southwest Radio Church tape, November, 1989.

5. Vitz, *Evidence of Bias in Our Children's Textbooks*, 84.

6. Mel and Norma Gabler, *What Are They Teaching Our Children?* (Victor Books), 164. Quoting from Public Law 95–561—November 1, 1978, Education Amendments of 1978, 20 USC 2701, "Protection of Pupil Rights," SEC 1250. Section 439 (b) 20 USC 1232h. The full amendment is available from Family Educational Rights and Privacy Act Office, U. S. Department of Education, 400 Maryland Ave., SW, Washington, D. C. 20202. This office also processes complaints.

7. Phyllis Schlafly, *Child Abuse in the Classroom* (Alton, Ill.: Pere Marquette Press, 1984).

8. Hermann Hesse, *Siddhartha* (New York: Bantam Books, 1981).

9. Wendy Flint, *A Call to Action* (American Freedom Coalition, 1988), 17.

10. Ann McFeatters, syndicated columnist in *Waterloo Courier* (September 27, 1989), D1.

11. Cliff Schimmels, *How to Help Your Child Survive and Thrive in Public School* (Old Tappan, N.J.:Fleming H. Revell, 1982).

12. "Focus on the Family" broadcast, November, 1989.

13. "Humanist touts accomplishments, asks for funds to win more victories," *American Family Association Journal* (May, 1989), 18.

14. John Eidsmoe, *The Christian Legal Advisor* (Milford, Mich.: Mott Media, Inc., 1984).

15. Russell Chandler, *Understanding the New Age* (Waco, Tex.: Word Publishing, 1988).

16. John W. Whitehead, *Parents' Rights* (Crossway Books, 1987).

17. Conversation with Ken Farnham, Pastor, First Christian Church, Cleveland, Okla. November, 1989.

18. School Library Bill of Rights, *Information Power* (Washington, D.C., 1988), 140.

19. People for the American Way, *Attacks on the Freedom to Learn, 49.*

20. Conversation with superintendent of schools Charles Clayton. Cleveland, Okla. November, 1989.

21. "How to Get Good Books in Your Local Library," Focus on the Family, *The Citizen Magazine* (August, 1988), 8.

22. *New Dimensions: The Psychology Behind the News,* (New Dimensions Publishing Co., Inc. 874 NE 7th St., Grants Pass, OR 97526–0069).

Chapter 7: From California to Ohio: What's in the Libraries and How Parents Helped Change Them

1. Letter from People for the American Way, November 5, 1990.

2. *Better Homes and Gardens* (September, 1990).

3. "How to Get Good Books in Your Local Library," *The Citizen* (August, 1988), 9.

Bibliography

American Family Association Journal. Drawer 2440, Tupelo, Miss. 38803. Published by Donald Wildmon.

American Library Association. *Booklist.*

American Library Association. *Information Power.* Chicago and London, and Washington, D. C.: The Association for Educational Communications and Technology, 1988. Current text for library science majors. Includes *Library Bill of Rights.*

Arbuthnot, May Hill. *Children and Books.* Chicago: Scott, Foresman and Co., 1964. College text used in the sixties and seventies.

Bender, David L., and Leone, Bruno, ser. eds.; O'Neill, Terry, book editor. *Censorship: Opposing Viewpoints.* St. Paul, Minn.: Greenhaven Press, 1985.

The Bible. Any translation.

Blackburn, William. "The Quest for Values in Contemporary American Fiction." Position paper at Canadian Council of Teachers of English. Saskatoon, Canada, August 15–20, 1982. Such position papers are usually available only at your college library: They mirror what professional teachers tell each other.

Bloom, Allan. *The Closing of the American Mind.* New York: Simon and Schuster, 1987.

Blumenfeld, Samuel. *NEA: Trojan Horse in American Education.* SW Radio Bible Church tapes. Box 1144, Oklahoma City, Okla. 1989.

Boer, Mark, ed. *Library Materials Guide.* Grand Rapids, Mich.: Christian Schools International, 1982–1989. One source of recommended teen fiction for Christian schools. Their sources include those which public schools implement.

Carlsen, G. Robert. *Books and the Teenage Reader*. New York: Harper and Row, 1967. One of the most respected teen-fiction experts' view of fiction just before it began its slide into valueless decision-making.

Chandler, Russell. *Understanding the New Age*. Dallas: Word Publishing, 1988. Handy encyclopedic format.

Christianity Today.

Citizen Magazine. Focus on the Family. Pomona, Calif. 91799.

Colson, Charles. *Kingdoms in Conflict*. New York: William Morrow (New York) and Zondervan (Grand Rapids, Mich.), 1987.

Concerned Women for America Magazine. 370 L'Enfant Promenade, S.W. Suite 800. Washington, D. C. 20035.

Dobson, Dr. James. *Fatal Addiction: Pornography and Sexual Violence*. Video or audio interview with Ted Bundy. Florida State Prison, January 23, 1989. Focus on the Family. Pomona, Calif. 91799.

The Education Reporter. Pere Marquette Press. Alton, Ill.

Eidsmoe, John. *The Christian Legal Advisor*. Milford, Mich.: Mott Media, Inc., 1984.

English Journal. National Council of Teachers of English. 1111 Kenyon Road, Urbana, Ill. 61801.

The Federal Register. September 6, 1984. Includes transcripts of Senate Hearings from parents in Orlando; Pittsburgh; Kansas City; Phoenix; Concord, N. H.; and Washington, D. C.

Fuchs, Lucy, Ph.D. "The Hidden Messages in Children's Books." Paper presented at Annual Meeting of Florida Reading Association, Jacksonville, Fla., October 18–21, 1984. Available in larger libraries.

Futas, Elizabeth. *Library Acquisition Policies and Procedures*. Oryx Press, Phoeniz, Ariz. 1977.

Gabler, Mel and Norma. *What Are They Teaching Our Children?* Wheaton, Ill.: Victor Books, 1985.

Gore, Tipper. *Raising PG Kids in an X-Rated Society*. Nashville: Abingdon Press, 1987.

Gow, Kathleen M., Ph.D. *Yes, Virginia, There Is Right and Wrong*. Wheaton, Ill.: Tyndale House, 1985.

Grant, George T. *Trial and Error: Understanding the American Civil Liberties Union.* Brentwood, Tenn.: Wolgemuth & Hyatt. 1989.

The Horn Book Magazine. Review source for librarians.

The Humanist Magazine.

Hunt, Gladys. *Honey for a Child's Heart.* Grand Rapids, Mich.: Zondervan, 1978.

Iowa Teen Award Annual Masterlist. Iowa Eductional Media Association. Available yearly at any Iowa public or school library.

Kilpatrick, William Kirk. *The Emperor's New Clothes.* Westchester, Ill.: Crossway Books, 1985.

Larrick, Nancy. *A Parent's Guide to Children's Reading.* Philadelphia: The Westminster Press, 1985.

National Council of Teachers of English, Donald R. Gallo, chair. *Books for You.* 1111 Kenyon Rd. Urbana, Ill. 1985.

New Dimensions Magazine: The Psychology Behind the News. 874 NE 7th St., Grants Pass, Oreg., 97526–0069.

New York State School Boards Association. *Textbook Selection: A Matter of Local Choice.* 119 Washington Ave., Albany, NY, 12210. 1988. Contact your state's school board association for one from your state.

The New York Times. Book Review Section.

Nilsen, Alleen Pace, and Donelson, Kenneth L. *Literature for Today's Young Adults,* 2nd ed. Glenview, Ill.: Scott, Foresman and Company, 1985. 3rd ed., 1989.

Parents' Choice Newsletter. Box 185. Waban, Mass., 02168.

People for the American Way. *Attacks on the Freedom to Learn.* 2000 M St., NW, Suite 400. Washington, D. C. 20036.

Publishers Weekly. "Hundreds of new books for the coming season chosen from publishers' lists." Reed Publishing. 249 W. 17th, New York NY 10011.

Pulling, Pat. *The Devil's Web.* Layfayette, La: Huntington House, 1989.

Ravitch, Diane, and Finn, Chester E., Jr. *What Do Our 17-Year-Olds Know?* New York: Harper and Row, 1987.

Reports of Committees 1989–90. Presented to the 69th Representative Assembly of the National Education Association. July 5–8, 1990. Kansas City, Mo.

Schaeffer, Dr. Francis. *The God Who Is There.* Downers Grove, Ill.: Inter-Varsity, 1968.

Schimmels, Cliff. *How to Help Your Child Survive and Thrive in the Public School.* Old Tappan, N.J.: Fleming H. Revell Co., 1982.

Schlafly, Phyllis. *Child Abuse in the Classroom.* Alton, Ill.: Pere Marquette Press, 1984.

School Library Journal. Reed Publishing. 249 W. 17th. New York, NY 10011.

Smith v. Board of School Com'rs of Mobile County, 655 F Supp. 939, S. D. Ala., 1987 ("Alabama Humanist Case").

Thomas, Cal. *Book Burning.* Westchester, Ill.: Crossway Books, 1983.

Thomas, Cal. *Occupied Territory.* Brentwood, Tenn.: Wolgemuth and Hyatt, 1987.

Toffler, Alvin. *Future Shock.* New York: Bantam Books, 1970.

Top of the News Magazine. A review source for librarians.

Vitz, Paul C. *Evidence of Bias in Our Children's Textbooks.* Ann Arbor, Mich.: Servant Books, 1986.

West, Mark I. *Trust Your Children.* New York: Neal-Schuman Publishers, Inc., 1988.

Wilson, Elizabeth. *Books Children Love.* Westchester, Ill.: Crossway Books, 1987.

Subject Index

About the Author

J ill Carlson grew up in northern Virginia, and then "just kept moving west." After receiving a Bachelor of Arts in English literature from Westminster College, New Wilmington, Pennsylvania, she taught English, drama, and speech full time in public schools. She taught private piano for seven years, and has substituted in secondary schools in Pennsylvania and Iowa. Raising parent awareness about local and national education issues is a top priority.

She considers her greatest accomplishment the full-time raising of her three children. She and her husband live on a farm near Cedar Falls, Iowa, where they test non-toxic cropping techniques. She has freelanced for newspapers and magazines. This is her first book.

The typeface for the text of this book is *Times Roman*. In 1930, typographer Stanley Morison joined the staff of *The Times* (London) to supervise design of a typeface for the reformatting of this renowned English daily. Morison had overseen type-library reforms at Cambridge University Press in 1925, but this new task would prove a formidable challenge despite a decade of experience in paleography, calligraphy, and typography. *Times New Roman* was credited as coming from Morison's original pencil renderings in the first years of the 1930s, but the typeface went through numerous changes under the scrutiny of a critical committee of dissatisfied *Times* staffers and editors. The resulting typeface, *Times Roman*, has been called the most used, most successful typeface of this century. The design is of enduring value to English and American printers and publishers, who choose the typeface for its readability and economy when run on today's high-speed presses.

Substantive Editing:
Michael S. Hyatt

Copy Editing:
Cynthia Tripp

Cover Design:
Steve Diggs & Friends
Nashville, Tennessee

Page Composition:
Xerox Ventura Publisher
Linotronic L-100 Postscript® Imagesetter

Printing and Binding:
Maple-Vail Book Manufacturing Group
York, Pennsylvania

Cover Printing:
Strine Printing Company
York, Pennsylvania